T0194957

Compelling! Elucidating! Demystifying! Dr. Raphael Thomas' major contribution on the subject of discipleship is a must-read for every Christian leader and believer involved in the Great Commission. *Congrats Bro. Raphael!*

Dr. Gerry O. Gallimore
former President/CEO YFC International,
Retired Senior Pastor Metropolitan Baptist Church,
Author of *Living By Faith*

If you want a journey through a full understanding of discipleship, *Demystifying Discipleship* is the perfect book. What I really appreciate about Dr. Thomas' approach is that the scope of the content is full, and the reader is led step-by-step from beginning to end.

One of the elements that delivers a connective thread is the arrangement and articulation of the chapters. The sections are thoughtful and smart and give an overarching succession that paints a bigger picture that is vital for the topic of discipleship.

In a church culture where there is a dangerous void of discipleship, *Demystifying Discipleship* is so critically important. Dr. Thomas has a passion for disciple-making and that passion comes through clearly through every page.

Dr. Steve McCoy
Lead Pastor, *The 360 Church,* Sarasota, FL
Founder, *SMALLCIRCLE*

Demystifying Discipleship is a passionate and urgent call to all Christians to engage in our primary mission of making disciples. Dr. Thomas' passion and experience in making disciples can be felt on every page, and not only inspires readers to get into action, but also provides them with practical steps to become effective disciple-makers.

Pastor Brian Grant
Germantown Christian Assembly
Philadelphia, Pennsylvania

This volume is about simplifying our understanding of Christian discipleship. Utilizing sound hermeneutical skills, Dr. Raphael Thomas carefully exegetes the critical biblical texts to establish the need for a shift in our thinking. This refreshing perspective on Discipleship is a must-read for astute Christians and scholars.

Dr. David Corbin
former President of the Caribbean Graduate School of Theology

Other books by the author

Biblical Dynamics for Revival Today: Lessons from the Life of King Hezekiah

From Nominal to Phenomenal: 14 Transformational Steps to Maximize Your Potential

Demystifying Discipleship

A Fresh Look at the Great Commission

Dr. Raphael J. Thomas

Foreword by Professor Dr. Arthur Dhanaraj

WESTBOW
PRESS®
A DIVISION OF THOMAS NELSON
& ZONDERVAN

WestBow Press books may be ordered through booksellers or by contacting:

WestBow Press
A Division of Thomas Nelson & Zondervan
1663 Liberty Drive
Bloomington, IN 47403
www.westbowpress.com
844-714-3454

605 E Mt Pleasant Avenue, Philadelphia Pennsylvania 19119
Email: raphaeljthomas@gmail.com

ISBN: 978-1-6642-4019-3 (sc)
ISBN: 978-1-6642-4020-9 (hc)
ISBN: 978-1-6642-4018-6 (e)

Library of Congress Control Number: 2021914102

Print information available on the last page.

WestBow Press rev. date: 10/20/2021

Dedicated to

My wife, Velda, and sons, Timothy and Nathanael,
and to all who are committed to the task
of making disciples of Jesus Christ.

CONTENTS

FOREWORD

I came to know Dr. Raphael Thomas closely while he was going through the equipping process to be an International Facilitator in 2008 though he had graduated from Haggai International in 2001. I have been watching his obedience to the Great Commission and leading others to obey it.

As a passionate Great Commission practitioner, Dr. Raphael has brought out the deep meaning and the process involved in disciple making through the analysis of the verses Mathew 28: 18-20. To me, this book is more than a fresh look at the Great Commission, it is a deeper insight that Dr. Raphael has brought out, investigating each aspect of the process of discipleship.

In the midst of hairsplitting arguments on evangelism versus discipleship, Dr. Raphael brought out beautifully the fabric of the Great Commission, woven with the threads that contribute to disciple making.

This book begins with a brief overview on the meaning, the marks, and the means of discipleship before demystifying discipleship.

The author brings in detail, the following steps, chapter-wise for effective discipleship: to appropriate God's power, appreciate God's priority, articulate God's plan, actuate God's process, assimilate God's people, accentuate God's *pre*-eminence, and anticipate God's presence. All these actions are explained in a lucid manner endorsed by Bible verses which makes it easier for every believer to understand and put into action.

As a theologian, Dr. Raphael has brought out the relevant scriptures rationally, even for a common man to comprehend and appreciate all the concepts and immerse with deeper discernments.

This book will be a great manual for every church member to be an effective disciple maker. I wish and pray that 'the body of Christ' will use it in their life groups and even the lessons can be passed on to the congregation from the pulpit so that we shall fill this earth with the disciples of Christ.

In the ministry of ending gospel poverty,

Dr. Arthur Dhanaraj
Chief Learning Officer
Haggai International

PREFACE

The substance of this book was first presented at the Annual Easter Convention of the Christian Brethren Assemblies Jamaica on April 2, 2018. It was one of the plenary presentations based on the theme "The Disciple-Making Church." My preparation for that presentation brought to a head a new passion that I had developed for discipleship the way Jesus practiced it.

This new passion was intensified by my exposure to Exponential, a church planting/church multiplication movement that annually hosts its main conference in Orlando, Florida. The Exponential movement has significantly fueled my fire for discipleship, through its plenary sessions and workshops, as well as training material that is made available through this ministry.

Another event that has contributed to this intensified passion for discipleship is a sobering experience that I had in February 2017 when I underwent quadruple heart bypass surgery. (I shared this testimony in my previous book: *From Nominal to Phenomenal: 14 Transformational Steps to Maximize Your Potential*). This passion led to the establishment of the missions organization *Blessing Basket International,* a nonprofit organization that is committed to partnering with churches and other organizations to help fulfill the Great Commission and promote the Great Commandments. This material is conceived as a training tool to rekindle flames and refuel fires for discipleship among individual believers, local churches, and even denominations "to make ready a people prepared for the Lord" (Luke 1:17). In fact, the title of this book was derived from the inaugural board meeting of Blessing Basket International (BBI) when Elder Alfred McDonald (now board chairman of BBI Jamaica) intimated that, for many persons, discipleship needs to be demystified. This is a humble attempt that I hope will contribute to both the *demystifying* and *doing* of discipleship.

I must also mention the impact of Haggai International on my life. I am constantly enriched and encouraged by the passion of Haggai International to end gospel poverty and make disciples of Jesus Christ. May we all join this noble endeavor to bring the gospel to those who have never heard. The unsaved and unreached are now everywhere, even your next-door neighbor. That is why contemporary missions must now be understood as "from everyone to everywhere"[1] and "from everywhere to everywhere"[2]

I am also grateful for the impact of Evangelism Explosion International on my life. This ministry also carries a great passion to share the gospel of Jesus Christ with clarity and confidence. I also thank the Lord for the Small Circle material that is produced by Pastor Steve McCoy. This tool has the added advantage of electronic and mobile applications.

I am also grateful for the Annotto Bay Gospel Chapel in St. Mary, Jamaica, and the North-Eastern Missionary Conference (a fellowship of thirty-three Christian Brethren Assemblies in northeastern Jamaica), which provided the immediate contexts to practice ministry for over thirty-two years. Much of the insights that I have gained over those precious years are distilled in this book.

This book is not intended to be a theological treatise on the Great Commission, although it *is* committed to sound biblical exegesis and exposition. It is primarily an inspirational and practical guide to enhance the task of making disciples of Jesus Christ among individual believers, churches, and para-church ministries.

It is my prayer that all who use this material will develop a passion for discipleship that is contagious, somewhat like COVID-19, except that it will bring new **life** instead of death. Please join me in prayer that the Lord will raise up many more persons to join in gathering the harvest, for "the harvest is plentiful, but the laborers are few" (Matthew 9:37). Discipleship begins with prayer. Jesus makes this clear in Matthew 9:35–38:

> Then Jesus went about all the cities and villages, teaching in their synagogues, preaching the gospel of the kingdom, and healing every sickness and every disease among the people. But when He saw the multitudes, He was moved with compassion for them, because they were weary and scattered, like sheep having no shepherd. Then He said to His disciples, "The harvest truly *is* plentiful, but the laborers *are* few. Therefore pray the Lord of the harvest to send out laborers into His harvest."

Let us hear and heed the word of Jesus again as recorded by the apostle John:

> Do you not say, "There are still four months and *then* comes the harvest"? Behold, I say to you, lift up your eyes and look at the fields, for they are already white for harvest! And he who reaps receives wages, and gathers fruit for eternal life, that both he who sows and he who reaps may rejoice together. For in this the saying is true: "One sows and another reaps." I sent you to reap that for which you have

not labored; others have labored, and you have entered into their labors. (John 4:35–38)

My brothers and sisters, the time of harvest is *now*. The harvest is ripe. When the harvest is ripe, it *cannot* wait. Will you be one of the harvesters?

ACKNOWLEDGMENTS

I would like to thank the many churches and organizations that have provided a platform for me to share the contents of this book. With each presentation, the material was further refined. In addition to various local churches, this material was presented at conferences hosted by the Christian Brethren Assemblies Jamaica (National Eastern Convention 2018), North-Eastern Missionary Conference, Jamaica (Missions Convention, October 2018) and Good Tidings Gospel Chapel, Brooklyn, New York (Memorial Day Conference 2019).

I would also like to thank Pastor Brian Grant and the leadership of the Germantown Christian Assembly (GCA), Philadelphia, Pennsylvania, for providing the opportunity to teach this material in a ten-week Bible study (Community Connections, fall 2020). Preparations for these studies added depth and breadth to the material. Thanks also to GCA for providing a context in which to practically engage in evangelism and discipleship as a member of its leadership team.

Much of the writing of this book was done while my family and I were in COVID lockdown in New York. Thanks to Barrington and Veronica Burt-Miller (my sister) and family for sharing their home with us during this period and for allowing their home to be used as our ministry center.

Thanks to all my teachers, mentors, relatives, prayer partners, and supporters who have helped to enhance our lives and ministry over the years.

Thanks also to my wife, Velda, and sons, Timothy and Nathanael, for your encouragement, inspiration, and love over the years.

Finally, I give thanks to God for granting grace and guidance to produce this book during times of turbulence caused by the COVID-19 and times of transition as my family was in the process of relocating from Jamaica to the USA to better position ourselves for global ministry.

I would also like to thank the team at Westbow Press for their guidance and assistance in completing this book.

INTRODUCTION

If one pericope in scripture succinctly encapsulates the mission and purpose of the church, it is the passage of scripture that is often referred to as the Great Commission, found in St. Matthew 28:16–20. This passage is also of paramount importance in helping us to understand what biblical discipleship entails. I know it is risky, if not seemingly presumptuous, to embark on a task of expounding such a familiar passage. However, I am prepared to take the risk with the conviction that the Holy Spirit is still able to give new illumination to his word and, more so, that the word of God cannot get stale:

> For the word of God *is* living and powerful, and sharper than any two-edged sword, piercing even to the division of soul and spirit, and of joints and marrow, and is a discerner of the thoughts and intents of the heart (Hebrews 4:12)

Also, sometimes the appeal of a meal is not only dependent on the ingredients it contains but on how it is prepared, packaged, and presented. I believe that the readers will develop a fresh appetite and aptitude for discipleship if they take the time to assimilate this material.

As mentioned above, the focus of this book is St. Matthew 28:16–20. However, we must also remember that the commission that Jesus gave to his disciples is recorded in all four gospels and Acts of the Apostles, and all are important for consideration in any discussion on discipleship. For your convenience I will list them all here.

> Then the eleven disciples went away into Galilee, to the mountain which Jesus had appointed for them. When they saw Him, they worshiped Him; but some doubted. And Jesus came and spoke to them, saying, "All authority has been given to Me in heaven and on earth. Go therefore and make disciples of all the nations, baptizing them in the name of the Father and of the Son and of the Holy Spirit, teaching them to observe all things that I have commanded you; and lo, I am with you always, even to the end of the age." Amen. (Matthew 28:16–20)

> Later He appeared to the eleven as they sat at the table; and He rebuked their unbelief and hardness of heart, because they did not believe those who had seen Him after He had risen. And He said to them, "Go into all the world and preach the gospel to every creature. He who believes and is baptized will be saved; but he who does not believe will be condemned. And these signs will follow those who believe: In My name they will cast out demons; they will speak with new tongues; they will take up serpents; and if they drink anything deadly, it will by no means hurt them; they will lay hands on

the sick, and they will recover." So then, after the Lord had spoken to them, He was received up into heaven, and sat down at the right hand of God. And they went out and preached everywhere, the Lord working with them and confirming the word through the accompanying signs. Amen. (Mark 16:14–20)

Then He said to them, "These are the words which I spoke to you while I was still with you, that all things must be fulfilled which were written in the Law of Moses and the Prophets and the Psalms concerning Me." And He opened their understanding, that they might comprehend the Scriptures. Then He said to them, "Thus it is written, and thus it was necessary for the Christ to suffer and to rise from the dead the third day, and that repentance and remission of sins should be preached in His name to all nations, beginning at Jerusalem. And you are witnesses of these things. Behold, I send the Promise of My Father upon you; but tarry in the city of Jerusalem until you are endued with power from on high. (Luke 24:46–48)

Then, the same day at evening, being the first day of the week, when the doors were shut where the disciples were assembled, for fear of the Jews, Jesus came and stood in the midst, and said to them, "Peace be with you." When He had said this, He showed them His hands and His side. Then the disciples were glad when they saw the Lord. So Jesus said to them again, "Peace to you! As the Father has sent Me, I also send you." And when He had said this, He breathed on them, and said to them, "Receive the Holy Spirit. If you forgive the sins of any, they are forgiven them; if you retain the sins of any, they are retained." (John 20:19–23)

And being assembled together with them, He commanded them not to depart from Jerusalem, but to wait for the Promise of the Father, "which," He said, "you have heard from Me; for John truly baptized with water, but you shall be baptized with the Holy Spirit not many days from now." Therefore, when they had come together, they asked Him, saying, "Lord, will You at this time restore the kingdom to Israel?" And He said to them, "It is not for you to know times or seasons which the Father has put in His own authority. But you shall receive power when the Holy Spirit has come upon you; and you shall be witnesses to Me in Jerusalem, and in all Judea and Samaria, and to the end of the earth." (Acts 1:4–8)

I share the sentiments of Jim Putman that there needs to be a major shift in how we do discipleship as he detailed in his book *Discipleshift*. He calls for a shift from reaching to making, from informing to equipping, from program to purpose, from activity to relationship, and from accumulating to deploying.[3]

I trust that this little book will help, even in some small way, to empower us to make the shift, even if we have settled for a long time. Faithfulness to God often calls us to shift the paradigm, shake the hegemony and shape new realities in discipleship. It is harvest time!

As we consider this vital theme of discipleship, it is important to give a brief overview of the topic. This overview will focus on the *meaning* of discipleship, the *marks* of discipleship and the *means* of discipleship.

The Meaning of Discipleship

The word *disciple* is from the Greek word *mathetes*, which generally refers to a "student" "pupil" "apprentice" or "adherent." According to Bible.org, a "disciple" is often associated with "people who were devoted followers of a great religious leader or teacher of philosophy."[4]

According to the *Cambridge Dictionary*, a disciple is "a person who believes in the ideas and principles of someone famous and tries to live the way that person does or did."[5] Therefore, a disciple is a person who is committed to following the teaching of Jesus Christ and imitating his life. One working definition of discipleship, given by Kenneth Ortiz is:

> Discipleship is the process a person goes through to go from being an unbeliever to a committed believer in Jesus Christ.[6]

The Marks of a Disciple

The Bible gives clear descriptions, even distinctions, of disciples. We will now consider three of the biblical marks of disciples.

1. Disciples Abide in the Word.

The word of God is the source of nourishment for the disciple of Jesus Christ, and so he must feed upon the word. St. John 8:31 underscores this point:

Then Jesus said to those Jews who believed Him, "If you abide in My word, you are My disciples indeed."

The Navigators, "an interdenominational ministry dedicated to evangelizing the lost and training Christians so that they, too, will disciple others"[7] uses an image of the hand to illustrate five ways how the word of God may be accessed. These include hearing, reading, studying, memorizing, and meditating. Each stage is important and is encouraged by scripture.[8] The disciple must hear the word, read the word, study the word, memorize the word, and meditate on the word of God to experience its transforming power.

2. Disciples Love One Another

Love is indeed a hallmark of the Christian life. Just as Christ loves us, we are called to love one another. This love is a distinguishing mark of the disciple. Jesus reiterates this when he declares:

> A new commandment I give to you, that you love one another; as I have loved you, that you also love one another.[35] By this all will know that you are My disciples, if you have love for one another." (John 13:34–35)

3. Disciples Bear Fruit

Another important distinguishing mark of the disciple is that disciples bear fruit. Jesus' first words to his disciples as well as his last words to them underscore this. When he first called his disciples, he said to them," Follow Me, and I will make you fishers of men" (Matthew 4:19). His final words to them were, "make disciples" (Matthew 28:19). It is clear from the word of God that we cannot be faithful disciples of Jesus Christ and **not** be interested in bearing fruits. Jesus says in John 15:8: "By this My Father is glorified, that you bear much fruit; so you will be My disciples."

If we truly desire to glorify God, we must be committed to fruit bearing. In the New Testament, fruit bearing is understood in various ways. We will now look at five ways in which fruit bearing is understood.

1. Christ-like life: A Christ-like life is associated with the fruit of the Spirit. Galatians 5:22–23 explains this:

> But the fruit of the Spirit is love, joy, peace, longsuffering, kindness, goodness, faithfulness, [23] gentleness, self-control. Against such there is no law.

2. Heartfelt praise: Praising God is considered as fruit in the life of a disciple.

> Therefore by Him let us continually offer the sacrifice of praise to God, that is, the fruit of *our* lips, giving thanks to His name. (Hebrews 13:15)

3. Financial generosity: Financial generosity is also regarded as fruit.

> Now you Philippians know also that in the beginning of the gospel, when I departed from Macedonia, no church shared with me concerning giving and receiving but you only. For even in Thessalonica you sent *aid* once and again for my necessities. "Not that I seek the gift, but I seek the fruit that abounds to your account. (Philippians 4:15–17)

4. Righteous conduct: Righteous conduct is a fruit. Disciples are expected to produce fruit worthy of repentance (Matthew 3:8).

> Now no chastening seems to be joyful for the present, but painful; nevertheless, afterward it yields the peaceable fruit of righteousness to those who have been trained by it (Hebrews 12:11).

5. Spiritual converts: Spiritual converts are also regarded as fruit.

> I urge you, brethren—you know the household of Stephanas, that it is the first fruits of Achaia, and *that* they have devoted themselves to the ministry of the saint (1 Corinthians 16:15).

So, we see it clearly in the Bible, a disciple must bear fruit—both qualitative and quantitative.

The Means of Discipleship

Let us consider some means of making disciples. This is important because sometimes it can be construed that one has to have a particular gift or personality type to be successful at making disciples. We will therefore explore some of the words that are used in the New Testament to emphasize the diversity of means that may be used to make disciples of Jesus Christ. We will highlight ten words that were used in the New Testament Greek and explain their meaning, most of which are listed in the Evangelism Training Association book *Your Ministry of Evangelism.*[9]

1. *Martureo*: **Witnessing**—sharing your experiences with others. Witness—one who shares what he has seen and heard (Acts 1:8).

2. *Leleo*: **Talking** to others (Acts 4:1).
3. *Euaggelizo*: **Evangelizing**—telling others about Christ; sharing good news (Acts 8:4).
4. *Didasko*: **Teaching**—systematic explanation (Matthew 28:20).
5. *Dialegomai*: **Reasoning**—answering reasonable objections (Acts 18:4, 1 Peter 3:15).
6. *Kataggello*: **Proclaiming**—declaring, lauding, celebrating (Acts 17:3, Colossians 1:28).
7. *Kerusso*: **Preaching**—announcing, heralding (Acts 8:5).
8. *Mathateuo*: **Discipling**—convincing others to follow Jesus (Matthew 28:19).
9. *Peitho*: **Persuading** those who are hesitant (2 Corinthians 5:11).
10. *Noutheteó*: **Admonishing**—warning, exhorting, counseling, reproving gently (Colossians 1:28).

The use of these many words show that a variety of strategies may be employed to make disciples of Jesus Christ. So, regardless of one's giftedness, personality style or personal preferences he or she can still be engaged in the task of making disciples.

Having looked at the meaning of disciple, some marks of the disciples and some means of making disciple, let us now proceed to take a more detailed look at the Great Commission, to demystify discipleship.

1

Appropriate God's Power

All authority has been given to me in heaven and
on earth.

—Matthew 28:18

It is not incidental or accidental that Jesus begins the Great
Commission by asserting his supreme authority. Discipleship can
only be carried out in God's power. It is important to understand
that the one who gave the commission to "make disciples," the
commissioner, is also the *creator* and *controller* of the universe (John
1:3; Colossians 1:16–17; Acts 17:24–26; Hebrews 1:3).

Jesus emphasized his supreme authority by asserting
unequivocally and unapologetically that "all authority is given
unto me" (Matthew 28:18). He undoubtedly wanted his disciples
to appreciate that the command to make disciples was given with
the full force of his authority. This is also underscored by Jesus'
use of the imperative mood in the Greek language. He used the

word *matheteusate,* which is a verb that means "make disciples" (Matthew 28:19). The imperative mood is a command mood. It is not a recommendation or a suggestion. It is a command! It is neither conditional nor optional. In fact, the only option that we have in the matter of making disciples is to obey or disobey. Jesus gives a command, and he expects us to obey his command, for he himself is the commander. It is a good time to examine yourself as you ask the question, Am I being obedient to my commander in chief in this matter of making disciples of Jesus Christ? The book of James reminds us that "to him who knows to do good and does not do *it,* to him it is sin" (James 4:17; italics added). This means that there can be sins of omission as well as sins of commission. Has the Great Commission become the Great Omission for you? If so, it is time to repent and renew your resolve to faithfully follow the commander who says, "Follow Me, and I will make you fishers of men" (Matthew 4: 19). If you are not engaged in fulfilling the Great Commission, you are committing a sin of omission. But God who calls us to make disciples also empowers us to make disciples, so we all can be engaged in the task of discipleship.

God's work can only be accomplished with God's power. In the Old Testament when Zerubbabel was called to rebuild the temple, he was told, "'Not by might nor by power, but by My Spirit,' Says the LORD of hosts" (Zechariah 4:6). Just like the building of the physical temple required the power of God, the building of the spiritual temple also requires the power of God. Disciple making requires the power of God because it is the building of the spiritual temple. It cannot be done by human skill or will. It is God alone who can save, and so we only work with him. The apostle Paul clarified this to the Thessalonians when he said,

For I determined not to know anything among you except Jesus Christ and Him crucified. I was with you in weakness, in fear, and in much trembling. And my speech and my preaching were not with persuasive words of human wisdom, but in demonstration of the Spirit and of power. (1 Corinthians 2:2–4)

If the building of the physical temple required the power of the Holy Spirit, then the building of the spiritual temple even more now requires the power of the Holy Spirit. The divine command for the followers of Jesus Christ to make disciples of all nations is consistent with another command: he "commands all men everywhere to repent" (Acts 17:30).

However, be assured that he who commands us to make disciples also promises that he himself will take the responsibility to "make" us fishers of people. "He who calls you *is* faithful, who also will do *it* (1 Thessalonians 5:24; italics added). So, like the apostle Paul we can say, "I have been crucified with Christ; it is no longer I who live, but Christ lives in me; and the *life* which I now live in the flesh I live by faith in the Son of God, who loved me and gave Himself for me" (Galatians 2:20; italics added). As we seek to make disciples of Jesus Christ we can affirm: I "labor, striving according to His working which works in me mightily" (Colossians 1:29).

The task of making disciples of Jesus Christ is firmly grounded in the sovereign authority of our Lord Jesus Christ. We must submit to that authority as well as serve in that authority. The task of making disciples of Jesus Christ is a divine mission and can only be carried out in the power of Jesus Christ. The apostle Paul, in celebration of the sovereign authority of Christ, stated:

Therefore God also has highly exalted Him and given Him the name which is above every name, that at the name of Jesus every knee should bow, of those in heaven, and of those on earth, and of those under the earth, and *that* every tongue should confess that Jesus Christ *is* Lord, to the glory of God the Father. (Philippians 2:9–11; italics added)

At the church planting and church multiplication conference that Exponential held in Florida in March 2018, church planter Samuel Stephens shared an experience in which he and his team went to minister in an unreached village in India. As they approached, one woman began to scream, "The Jesus people are coming. I have to leave this village." They entered the village and delivered the woman, who was demonized, and established a local church in the name and power and authority of Jesus Christ, for the commission to make disciples is in the authority of Jesus Christ. He affirms boldly, "All authority is given unto me" (Matthew 2:18).

It is important to underscore the authority of Jesus Christ in the mission of making disciples because an active and relentless enemy is persistently opposing the task of making disciples. Jesus assures us that he will build his church, and the gates of hell cannot prevail against it (Matthew 16:18).

When he sent out his disciples on the mission, he told them:

Behold, I give you the authority to trample on serpents and scorpions, and over all the power of the enemy, and nothing shall by any means hurt you. (Luke 10:19)

When the disciples returned from their mission and gave their victorious report, Jesus acknowledged, "I saw Satan fall like lightning from heaven" (Luke 10:18). The early church had to wait for the *sound* from heaven and the *fire* from heaven. Jesus had promised his followers that he would empower them before they took up the job of making disciples.

I believe that this power helps us overcome our own fear and apathy as well as the satanic oppositions to disciple making. Praise the Lord, Jesus Christ has spoiled (disarmed) principalities and powers and made a show of them, openly triumphing over them in the cross (Colossians 2:15).

Songwriters Carolyn Cross and Phil Cross express it well:

He is higher than the highest,

Greater than the great,

No one will ever take His crown away;

He's more mighty than mightiest,

He reigns from above,

He's the all-time, undisputed, undefeated,

Champion of love.[10]

It is not surprising, then, to note that Jesus exhorted his disciples to go to Jerusalem and wait to be empowered from on high before they embarked on the mission of making disciples. Let us hear the Word of God again:

"For John truly baptized with water, but you shall be baptized with the Holy Spirit not many days from now." Therefore, when they had come together, they asked Him, saying, "Lord, will You at this time restore the kingdom to Israel?" And He said to them, "It is not for you to know times or seasons which the Father has put in His own authority. But you shall receive power when the Holy Spirit has come upon you; and you shall be witnesses to Me in Jerusalem, and in all Judea and Samaria, and to the end of the earth." (Acts 1:5–8)

This promise was fulfilled in Acts chapter 2 when the church was baptized in the Holy Ghost. The church received power to bear witness of Christ when it received the Holy Spirit. We can only be faithful and fruitful disciple makers when we have received power from God's Spirit.

Understanding the Meaning of Authority

What really is the meaning of "authority"? The *Baker's Evangelical Dictionary of Biblical Theology*[11] gives the following explanations:

1. Authority is the freedom to decide or a right to act without hindrance.
2. Authority refers to the power, ability, or capability to complete an action.
3. The word "authority" is used with reference to delegated authority in the form of a warrant, license, or authorization to perform.
4. Authority sometimes denotes the sphere in which authority is exercised (e.g., civil government, jurisdiction).

Ten Ways to Appropriate the Authority of Christ

Mission mobilizer Dr. Paul Borthwick, who serves as a senior consultant for Development Associates International and teacher at Gordon College in Massachusetts, captures the importance of authority well in the following statement:

> The resurrected Jesus begins by establishing our *platform* for outreach: his supreme authority. "*All* authority" is his. Our commission into the world is not denominational or local church based. It is not primarily motivated by human need or by strategic opportunity. We're sent out by the authority of Jesus. And it's no small authority—in heaven and on earth.
>
> Knowing that we stand on his authority gives us boldness to speak (look at the disciples in the book of Acts). It gives us courage to realize that the authority behind us is the power that raised Jesus from the dead. It empowers us to address the pluralistic spirit that proclaims all "truths" are equal and none are absolute. When we go out in outreach and proclamation to others, we stand on the superlative authority of Jesus.[12]

Let us now look at ten ways in which we may appropriate the authority of Christ in the task of making disciples. Sometimes the word *power* is used interchangeably with *authority* and so for our purposes here we will use the word *power*.

1. Appropriate the Power of the Word

The Bible tells us in Hebrews 4:12 the word of God is "quick" and "powerful." That means that it is "living" and "active" in that it contains "life" and "energy." Inherent in the word of God is a dynamite that propels us to accomplish the will of God. The Lord asks the questions to iterate the point, "*Is* not My word Like afire?"…"And like a hammer *that* breaks the rock in pieces?" (Jeremiah 23:29). Paul tells us that the word of God is the "sword of the Spirit" (Ephesians 6:17). It is the word of God that the Holy Spirit uses to cause conviction and conversion. Therefore, as we seek to make disciples of Jesus Christ, we must arm ourselves with the sword of the Spirit.

2. Appropriate the Power of the Holy Spirit
    Jesus made it clear that the task of making disciples is dependent upon the power of the Holy Spirit.

    But you shall receive power when the Holy Spirit has come upon you; and you shall be witnesses to Me in Jerusalem, and in all Judea and Samaria, and to the end of the earth. (Acts 1:8)

    The disciples were instructed to wait in Jerusalem until they were endued with power from on high (Acts 1:5).

    *   To appropriate the power of the Holy Spirit we must have a correct relation with him. Three things are important in this respect.
        a. "Do not quench the Spirit" (1 Thessalonians 5:19). This means that we must not extinguish the fire of the Holy Spirit. We must not dismiss or resist the promptings of the Holy Spirt when he guides us to make disciples, or to do anything for that matter.

b. The Bible also exhorts us: Do not grieve the Spirit. "And do not grieve the Holy Spirit of God, by whom you were sealed for the day of redemption" (Ephesians 4:30). Since the Holy Spirit is God and has emotions, we should refrain from engaging in those things that hurt the Holy Spirit. Sin in the lives of believers causes grief to the Holy Spirit.

c. Be filled with the Spirit. "Be filled with the Spirit" (Ephesians 5:8). We are encouraged to be totally controlled by the Spirit, even as too much wine causes significant influence on persons. "And do not be drunk with wine, in which is dissipation; but be filled with the Spirit." (Ephesians 5:18).

3. Appropriate the Power of the Blood

As we make disciples, we must appropriate the power of the blood of Jesus Christ. Since the making of disciples is constantly opposed by Satan and his emissaries, we need to overcome him constantly as we engage in making disciples. We overcome by appealing to the blood of the Lamb since Satan has already been defeated at the cross of Jesus Christ.

> And they overcame him by the blood of the Lamb and by the word of their testimony, and they did not love their lives to the death. (Revelation 12:11)

The blood of the Lamb protected the children of Israel when the angel of death was passing over Egypt. Exodus 12:13 tells us:

> Now the blood shall be a sign for you on the houses where you *are*. And when I see the blood, I will pass

over you; and the plague shall not be on you to destroy *you* when I strike the land of Egypt.

The blood of Jesus Christ still provides protection for the children of God. There is still power in the blood of Jesus Christ although it was shed some two thousand years ago. The victory that was secured by the death of Jesus Christ must constantly be affirmed as we make disciples of Christ. This is because it is through the death of Jesus Christ that the plans of Satan were destroyed and he himself was disarmed.

> Inasmuch then as the children have partaken of flesh and blood, He Himself likewise shared in the same, that through death He might destroy him who had the power of death, that is, the devil, and release those who through fear of death were all their lifetime subject to bondage. (Hebrews 2:14–15)

> Having disarmed principalities and powers, He made a public spectacle of them, triumphing over them in it. (Colossians 2:15)

4. Appropriate the Power of the Name of Jesus
   We can also appropriate the authority of Jesus Christ by using the *name* of Jesus. There is power in the name of Jesus. Paul speaks about the power of the name of Jesus in Philippians 2:8–11:

> And being found in appearance as a man, He humbled Himself and became obedient to *the point of* death, even the death of the cross. Therefore God also has highly exalted Him and given Him the

name which is above every name, that at the name of Jesus every knee should bow, of those in heaven, and of those on earth, and of those under the earth, and *that* every tongue should confess that Jesus Christ *is* Lord, to the glory of God the Father.

Peter and John ministered healing to a crippled man by appealing to the name of Jesus.

> Then Peter said, "Silver and gold I do not have, but what I do have I give you: In the name of Jesus Christ of Nazareth, rise up and walk. And he took him by the right hand and lifted *him* up, and immediately his feet and ankle bones received strength. (Acts 3:6–7)

Apostle Paul cast out demons in the name of Jesus. One example is that of the girl who had a spirit of divination.

> And this she did for many days. But Paul, greatly annoyed, turned and said to the spirit, "I command you in the name of Jesus Christ to come out of her." And he came out that very hour. (Acts 16:18)

5. Appropriate the Power of Prayer
   Another way we can appropriate the power of God in the process of disciple making is to make use of the privilege of prayer. We must pray earnestly for the persons we seek to disciple. Jesus prayed earnestly for his disciples (John 17). The apostle Paul prayed earnestly for the church (Philippians1:9–11; Ephesians 1:15–23, 3:14–21). We are called to pray for one another.

It was the power of prayer that caused the early church to survive intense persecution. Even when their lives were threatened, they continued to pray. Acts 4:31 records:

> And when they had prayed, the place where they were assembled together was shaken; and they were all filled with the Holy Spirit, and they spoke the word of God with boldness.

Again, in Acts 12 we see the power of prayer demonstrated in the early church. James was killed, and when Herod saw that it pleased the people, he was planning to do the same with Peter. But prayer made a difference. In Acts 12:5 the scriptures record:

> Peter was therefore kept in prison, but constant prayer was offered to God for him by the church.

As a result of those constant prayers, God sent his angels into the prison, who awakened Peter, released him from the chains, passed the soldiers, open the iron gates, and led Peter out of prison. The power of prayer was unleashed because of persistent and consistent prayer.

6. Appropriate the Power of Sonship
   We can also appropriate the power of Christ by appealing to our relationship as children of God. People of God are *bona fide* members of the family of God, and that brings power with it. St. John 1:12 states:

> But as many as received him, to them gave he power to become the sons of God, even to them that believe on his name. (KJV)

Here it is clear that believers have the "power" or right to be called the children of God. As children of God, we are new creatures (2 Corinthians 5:17). This new birth came about by the resurrection power of Jesus Christ. In other words, believers have access to the resurrection power of Jesus Christ, evidenced by the new birth (Romans 6:4–6). It was Paul's desire that he might experience the "power of his resurrection" (Philippians 3:120). In fact, he tells the Ephesian church that the same power that raised Jesus from the dead is at work in us mightily (Ephesians 1:19–21). So, when we engage in the task of making disciples of Jesus Christ, we can be assured that we do so in the resurrection power of Jesus Christ, or what I call the power of sonship, the power of the life of Christ that is working in us. We are legitimate children of God.

> and if children, then heirs—heirs of God and joint heirs with Christ, if indeed we suffer with *Him,* that we may also be glorified together. (Romans 8:17)

7. Appropriate the Power of Apostleship

We can also appropriate the authority of Christ when we understand that we are sent by him. We use the term "apostleship" here to refer to our "sent-ness." We are a *sent* people. We are on God's mission in the world. We did not embark on the task of disciple making on our own. It is in direct obedience to a divine command. When Christ sends us out to make disciples, he also gives us delegated authority. The fact that we are ambassadors of Christ (2 Corinthians 5:20) means that we have the backing of the kingdom of God. As ambassadors of Christ we have the authority to represent Christ in this world.

8. Appropriate the Power of our Position in Christ

 Another thing that will help us to appropriate the authority of Christ in disciple making is to understand our position in Christ. According to the Bible we are raised up and made to sit in heavenly places in Christ Jesus (Ephesians 2:6). Christ himself is seated at the right hand of God in heavenly places (Ephesians 1:20). Moreover, our lives are hidden together with Christ in God. So, we are not only *risen* with Christ, but we are also *hidden* in Christ (Colossians 3:1–3). The very thought that we are seated with Christ positionally in heavenly places should underscore the authority with which we are equipped to make disciples of Jesus Christ.

9. Appropriate the Power of the Christian Armor

 Another way to ensure that we appropriate the authority of Christ is to put on the full armor of God. The Bible tells us in Ephesians 6:10: "Finally, my brethren be strong in the Lord and in the power of His might" (Ephesians 10:10). We are strong, even powerful, when we are clothed in the full armor of God. Note the three words used in this verse: "power," "strong," and "might."

In this passage seven pieces of the armor are identified. These are:

    a. the belt of truth
    b. the breastplate of righteousness
    c. shield of faith
    d. helmet of Salvation
    e. the sword of the Spirit
    f. feet shod with the preparation of the gospel of peace
    g. prayers and supplication

Discipleship involves warfare and therefore we need to make use of the weapons that the Lord has provided for us. Spiritual work requires spiritual weapons.

> For the weapons of our warfare *are* not carnal but mighty in God for pulling down strongholds. (2 Corinthians 10:4)

Jesus taught that we cannot plunder a strong man's house without first binding the strong man (Mark 3:27). Discipleship is tantamount to plundering Satan's kingdom. Therefore, evangelism and discipleship must not be entered casually or carelessly. They involve spiritual warfare and must make appropriate use of the spiritual armor provided by God.

10. Appropriate the Power of Our Testimony
We can also appropriate the authority of Christ by using our testimony. Telling of what Christ has done for us can be a powerful tool to make disciples of Jesus Christ. Revelation 12:11 tells us:

> and they overcame him by the blood of the lamb
> and by the word of their testimony, and they did not
> love their lives to the death.

Jesus said that his disciples would be witnesses of him when they received the power of the Holy Spirit (Acts 1:8). A witness is someone who bears testimony. We must be willing to share the good things that God has done for us as we seek to make disciples of Jesus Christ, for our testimony can be a powerful tool in the hand of a mighty God.

So, we see in this chapter that we are sent out by Jesus with his authority to make disciples. We must, therefore, take the courageous step to obey and appropriate the authority of Christ himself to make disciples, since we are furnished with the powerful spiritual resources to do so.

2

Appreciate God's Priority

"Go therefore and *make disciples* of all the nations."
(Italics added.)

—Matthew 28:19

Inasmuch as the text calls us to *appropriate God's power in discipleship,* I believe it also calls us to *appreciate God's priority for discipleship.* I believe that the priority of disciple making can be substantiated by at least four proofs. These are the explicit command of Jesus, the example of Jesus himself, the example and teaching of the apostles, and the evidence of church history. We will briefly consider these.

The Explicit Command of Jesus

As pointed out earlier, at the heart of the Great Commission passage is the word *matheteusate,* which means "to make disciple." It is the leading verb, and the only verb, in the passage. The other verbal forms in the passage are *going, baptizing,* and *teaching.* These are participles and hang on the leading verb. The importance of making disciples is underscored by the imperative mood; that is, the command mood. Hence, the task of making disciples is a nonnegotiable for those who follow Jesus Christ. The last command that Jesus gave to his followers was forceful and deliberate. It is also interesting to note that the last words of Jesus Christ to his disciples (the commission passage) are consistent with his first words to them: "Follow Me, and I will make you fishers of men" (Matthew 4:19). Therefore, it is evident that our calling is bound up with our commission. The very grammatical and syntactical arrangement of the passage endorses the priority of making disciples in God's agenda.

Even the words used to describe followers of Christ place an emphasis on the word *disciple*. In his book *Disciples that Make Disciples: Twelve Lessons in Biblical Discipleship,* Joe Wyrostek points out the word *Christian* is only mentioned three times in the Bible, the word *believer* is mentioned around twenty-six times, but the word *disciple* is found over 250 times. He goes on to explain that this "choice of words makes it clear how Jesus wants us to identify ourselves. He wants us to be his disciples."[13]

The Example of Jesus

God's priority for making disciples is also underscored by the example set by Jesus himself, our model of ministry. When Jesus came to this earth his ministry was heavily focused on discipleship. The Bible tells us that "He appointed twelve, that they might be with Him and that He might send them out to preach, and to have power to heal sicknesses and to cast out demons" (Mark 3:14–15). Inasmuch as Jesus was concerned about the multitude, he chose twelve men to give intensive training. Jesus operated in concentric circles. He had an inner circle of three friends, Peter, James, and John. Then he had the twelve disciples. This is followed by the seventy-two disciples that he sent out to minister and the 120 who waited in the upper room in Jerusalem for the outpouring of the Holy Spirit. He had the five hundred whom he appeared to personally after his resurrection, and he had the thousands that he taught, fed, and healed in his ministry. Yet unquestionably Jesus spent the greater part of his ministry preparing disciples to continue the work he started. Jesus' major strategy to spread the good news of the kingdom is to invest in the lives of others who would multiply the impact of his ministry. This, indeed, is exponential impact.

It is noticeably clear from the gospel narratives that a priority of Jesus's earthly ministry was to prepare his disciples. He prayerfully and deliberately chose twelve men whom he gave intensive training to carry out his ministry. He could have chosen any strategy, but he set the example for us of intensive discipleship of some while we still touch the lives of the multitude. As a result of the early disciples, Christianity is currently the religion with the most adherents in the world today.

The Example and Teaching of the Apostles

The disciples themselves became disciple makers. They went to various territories preaching the gospel, but they also gave special attention to those who would become leaders in the ministry. Apostle Paul, who was not one of the original twelve disciples but was chosen as an apostle to the Gentiles, also gave priority to disciple making. He not only practiced it, but he taught it. He absorbed God's priority of discipleship in his own life and ministry. He exhorted Timothy to do the same:

> And the things that you have heard from me among
> many witnesses, commit these to faithful men who
> will be able to teach others also. (2 Timothy 2:2)

He also admonished the Corinthian church with the words, "Imitate me, just as I also *imitate* Christ" (1 Corinthians 11:1).

The Evidence of Church History

Another factor that affirms the priority of discipleship in God's agenda is the success of churches and organizations that intentionally practice discipleship. One phenomenon that captures the success of the church is revival or spiritual renewals/awakenings.

The prominence of prayer and preaching in revivals is often celebrated, but we mut not forget the place of personal discipleship in sustaining revivals.

In his book *Marks of a Movement: What the Church Today Can Learn from the Wesleyan Revival,* Winfield Bevins advocates:

> One of the great lessons we are reminded of by the Wesleyan revival is that the purpose of the church is to make disciples. Perhaps more than anything, it was the *intentional* discipleship systems that contributed to the growth and longevity of the movement. One obvious reason so many churches struggle with making disciples is that they do not have a plan for it. In addition, many church leaders have not personally experienced what it is to live in healthy Christian community. Wesley reminds us that when these things are lost, the church must endeavor to rediscover the power of biblical Christian community.[14]

The benefits of having a conscientious and consistent focus on making disciples in churches can be seen in the example of one such organization—Evangelism Explosion (EE). EE was started by

Dr. D. James Kennedy in 1962 while pastoring at the Coral Ridge Presbyterian Church, Fort Lauderdale, Florida. According to the EE website, Dr. Kennedy had become discouraged because of the decline in number of his congregants. He is quoted as saying,

> "Extrapolation made it clear that I had two-and-a-half months of ministry left before I was preaching to only my wife—and she was threatening to go to the Baptist Church down the street!"[15]

However, around that time he had the opportunity to watch a friend, Pastor Kennedy Smartt, do evangelism in Georgia. Within ten days, fifty-four people made professions of faith in Christ. That experience rekindled new hope for him. He went back to his home church and developed a systematic method of sharing the gospel, which later developed into Evangelism Explosion. His church began to experience tremendous growth so that "in a brief 12-year period, church membership increased from 17 to 2,000."[16] Such is the impact of consistent discipleship.

It is true that God is interested in all human life. He is concerned about the physical well-being of people. He is also concerned about the social and emotional stability of individuals and communities. He cares about the good will of nations and the environment. However, it is God's priority is to make disciples. He commands all people everywhere to repent (Acts 17:30). He is "not willing that any should perish but that all should come to repentance" (2 Peter 3:9). If this is true, it should be instructive in how the church orders its priorities. Jesus left heaven and came to earth to die for lost sinners so that people may be forgiven for their sins, find eternal life, and be prepared to spend eternity with him. Whatever else we do as disciples of Jesus Christ, me must ensure that we offer to people the gift of God, which is eternal life (Romans 3:23).

Sometimes, the church can get terribly busy with activities that are far removed from God's priority. Whatever the church does must strategically contribute in some way to the task of making and maturing disciples of Jesus Christ. May we truly demonstrate that we appreciate God's priority for discipleship.

3

Articulate God's Plan

"All authority … all nations …all things that I have
commanded …with you always."

—Matthew 28:18–20

So far, we have seen that the Great Commission calls us to appropriate
God's power in discipleship and appreciate God's priority in
discipleship. I would also like to suggest that if we are going to be
faithful disciples of Jesus Christ, we must articulate God's plan for
discipleship. When we understand God's plan, we can play our part
in fulfilling that plan.

I believe that we can summarize God's plan for discipleship with
the words *compulsory* and *comprehensive.*

Compulsory Plan

It has already been pointed out that the task to make disciples is
written in the imperative. It is mandatory. Disciples do not have the

option to determine if they should participate in making disciples. They either obey or disobey. If we are followers of Jesus Christ, disciple making is a part of our job description. It is not an elective. It is a part of the core curriculum. If you are leaving it out of your action plan, you are missing the mark.

In our fast-paced world (except in COVID-19 times) we often get swamped with activities. The sad reality is that sometimes we engage in those activities without engaging in disciple making. Sometimes we major on the minors. Sometimes we substitute the peripheral for the primary and the urgent for the important. We must remember that we are called to be "fishers of men" and not just "feeders of fish." Sometimes the ministry can be so packaged that it is nothing more than entertainment. Sometimes, there is much bait but no hook. It may be great to use many and varied baits, but the hook must also be present. The hook is the unadulterated gospel of Jesus Christ, for it alone is the power of God unto salvation (Romans 1:16). Whatever else we do as disciples of Jesus Christ, we must also remember that we are commanded to make disciples. It is compulsory. In fact, it is *the* job description for the church.

Comprehensive Plan

One of the interesting features of the Great Commission passage in Matthew is the emphasis on the word *all*, which is used three times.

First, the word *all* is used in reference to "all power" that has been given to Jesus Christ. Since this has already been dealt with in chapter 1, I will not repeat it here.

Second, the word *all* is also used with reference to "teaching" disciples "to observe *all* things" (Matthew 28:18–19) that the Lord has commanded. This aspect of the great commission will be dealt with in chapter 4, so here is a chance to be a good disciple and exercise the virtue called patience. Third, the great commission calls us to make disciples of "all nations." The Greek expression for this is *panta ta ethne* (all the nations). The word *nations* here refers to people groups. One nation may be made up of many people groups. It is God's plan for all people groups to hear the message of the gospel. For example, according to the Joshua Project[17], India alone has 2,717 people groups and China has 544 people groups. What the scripture is referring to here is ethnic groups. It is God's plan for disciples to be made among all the ethnic groups in the world. It is a comprehensive plan.

From the dawn of creation, God's plan is a global plan. From Genesis to Revelation, God is interested in all the nations. This global theme is developed throughout the Bible. The global plan of God for the salvation of the nations can be summed up in the following major moves:

1. Creation
2. Catastrophe
3. Call of Abraham
4. Carrying out of bondage
5. Consolidation of a nation
6. Coming of Messiah
7. Commission of Christ
8. Church on mission
9. Consummation of our salvation

Here is an abbreviated overview of the development of God's global plan revealed in the Bible.[18]

Creation

When God created the heavens and the earth, everything was good. When he created human beings, he said it was "very good." He blessed humanity and gave the command to "fill the earth" and subdue it. From then, it was a global plan. Genesis 1:28 says:

> Then God blessed them, and God said to them, "Be fruitful and multiply; fill the earth and subdue it; have dominion over the fish of the sea, over the birds of the air, and over every living thing that moves on the earth."

Catastrophe

By Genesis 3, the entire creation became impacted by sin and its consequence: death. Romans 5:12 tells us:

> Through one man sin entered the world, and death through sin, and thus death spread to all men, because all sinned.

However, in the same chapter that records the impact of sin on the world, God revealed the seed of the plan for redemption, referred to as *protoevangelium*, meaning first evangelism. This is revealed in Genesis 3:15 and is regarded as the earliest messianic promise in scripture. Genesis 3:15 reads:

> And I will put enmity

> Between you and the woman,

> And between your seed and her Seed;

> He shall bruise your head,

> And you shall bruise His heel.

So, from Genesis, God had a plan to redeem fallen humanity. This continued to be developed in the biblical narrative.

The impact of sin on humans was so severe that God had to destroy the entire world in the flood, saving only Noah and his family in the ark, for he "found grace in the eyes of the Lord" (Genesis 6:8).

After the flood, the earth got a fresh start and again,

> God blessed Noah and his sons, and said to them:
> "Be fruitful and multiply, and fill the earth."
> (Genesis 9:1)

Yet, humans continued to rebel against God by trying to reach up to heaven by themselves or making a name for themselves, but God would have none of it. He demolished their selfish ambitions, destroyed the tower of Babel, and dispersed them (Genesis 11), for God's plan is a global plan. Following on the heels of that story, God called Abraham to declare his name to the nations.

Call of Abraham

God chose to call a man by the name of Abraham to begin his global plan to reach the nations. The Bible tells us that the Lord had said to Abram (before his name was changed to Abraham):

> "Get out of your country,
>
> From your family
>
> And from your father's house,
>
> To a land that I will show you.

I will make you a great nation;

I will bless you

And make your name great;

And you shall be a blessing.

I will bless those who bless you,

And I will curse him who curses you;

And in you all the families of the earth shall

be blessed." (Genesis 12:1–3)

Abraham was called to be blessed and to be a blessing to the nations, not to hug up the blessing for himself but to be a conduit of blessing to the nations of the earth. God made a covenant with Abraham to give him the land of Israel (Canaan) and make him the father of a great nation. He became the father of the Jewish people, who were enslaved in Egypt for four hundred years.

Carrying Out of Bondage

God, according to his plans, carried the children of Israel "out of Egypt with a mighty hand and an outstretched arm, with great terror and with signs and wonders" (Exodus 3:8) to the promised land. They were promised blessing if they obeyed the Lord and served him faithfully because they were consolidated as a nation special to God, so that they could be a light to the nations and be the medium through which salvation would come to fallen humanity.

Consolidation of a Nation

God established the nation of Israel as a pivotal part of his plan to bless the nations. The prophet Isaiah, like many of the prophets, declared the word of the Lord to Israel:

> I am the LORD; I have called you in righteousness; I will take you by the hand and keep you; I will give you as a covenant for the people, a light for the nations. (Isaiah 42:6)

> It is too light a thing that you should be my servant to raise up the tribes of Jacob and to bring back the preserved of Israel; I will make you as a light for the nations, that my salvation may reach to the end of the earth. (Isaiah 49:6)

The Israelites lived in the land and enjoyed the blessing of the Lord, but when they rebelled against the Lord, they were taken away from their homeland by the Assyrians and the Babylonians. But the forgiving God brought them back to their homeland after seventy years in exile.

Coming of Messiah

Despite the instability and unfaithfulness of Israel, God still brought his promise to pass by sending the Messiah as a descendant of Abraham who would bring blessing to the world. The apostle Paul declares:

> But when the fullness of the time had come, God sent forth His Son, born of a woman, born under the law, to redeem those who were under the law, that

we might receive the adoption as sons. (Galatians 4:4-5)

This special relationship with the Father was not confined to a particular nation or culture. It was available to all who believe in Jesus Christ the Messiah.

> But as many as received Him, to them He gave the right to become children of God, to those who believe in His name (John 1:12).

> For the grace of God that brings salvation has appeared to all men, teaching us that, denying ungodliness and worldly lusts, we should live soberly, righteously, and godly in the present age, looking for the blessed hope and glorious appearing of our great God and Savior Jesus Christ, who gave Himself for us, that He might redeem us from every lawless deed and purify for Himself His own special people, zealous for good works. (Titus 2:11)

So, there we have it. Jesus the Messiah came from heaven with a message of salvation (deliverance) for all peoples. He called and trained his disciples and commissioned them to take the gospel to all the world. He gave his own life to pay the price of sin and rose again from the dead to conquer death and hell and guarantee new life in God. He went back to heaven to sit at the Father's right hand.

Commission of Christ

However, before he left, he gave his followers the command to make disciples of all nations. This is what we have been exploring. From heaven, he poured out the Holy Spirit to reside in all who accept his salvation and empower them to be his witnesses to all nations.

> But you shall receive power when the Holy Spirit
> has come upon you; and you shall be witnesses to
> Me in Jerusalem, and in all Judea and Samaria, and
> to the end of the earth" (Acts 1:8)

Jesus gave this global assignment to the church, which is made up of all his followers.

The Church on Mission

This global mission of the church must be accomplished between the return of Jesus to heaven and his second coming. He is coming to consummate our salvation and usher in the eternal state. Some will be with him, and some will be separated into eternal damnation.

The only hope for persons to receive eternal salvation is through Jesus Christ who alone can save humankind from sin.

> Nor is there salvation in any other, for there is no
> other name under heaven given among men by
> which we must be saved. (Acts 4:12)

He gave his followers the commission to every nation because he commands all men everywhere to repent (Acts 17:31).

It is the purpose of the church now to take the gospel to the ends of the earth. Jesus himself promised that he will build his church and not even the gates of hell shall prevail against it (Matthew 16:18). Missions to the nations is what sets the agenda of the church. When the mission of the church is complete, our Lord Jesus will return.

Consummation of Salvation

Christ will return for a church that is made up of people drawn from the ends of the earth. Apostle John was given a revelation of this group in the celestial kingdom and writes:

> After these things I looked, and behold, a great multitude which no one could number, of all nations, tribes, peoples, and tongues, standing before the throne and before the Lamb, clothed with white robes, with palm branches in their hands. (Revelation 7:9)

O what a glory that will be when all God's children are gathered around the throne of God worshipping in that eternal state.

Reverting to the comprehensive nature of the Great Commission, I would also like to underscore that the task to make disciples of Jesus Christ was not only given to the twelve disciples only, or the seventy-two disciples only or the over five hundred persons that the resurrected Lord appeared to before he ascended to heaven. The commission is to *all* the followers of Jesus Christ. All who have received the gift of the Holy Spirit are empowered to bear witness of Jesus Christ. Again, the word of God says:

> But you shall receive power when the Holy Spirit has come upon you; and you shall be witnesses to Me in Jerusalem, and in all Judea and Samaria, and to the end of the earth. (Acts 1:8)

Again, according to the Joshua Project, of the world's 7.5 billion people in the word today, 2.17 billion have had virtually no exposure to the gospel.[19] In terms of Bible translation, of the 7,360 languages spoken today only 2,252 have the New Testament available (covering

90 percent of the world's population). Although God is doing phenomenal things around the world, there is still much work to be done to fulfill the Great Commission. By the way, if God is calling you to become more deliberate in participating in global evangelization, please do not resist him. Just stop for a moment, yield yourself to him, and pray that he will show you clearly how you can help to fulfill the Great Commission. There is a work that you can do!

4

Actuate God's Process

Teaching them to observe all things that I have commanded you.

—Matthew 28:20

It must not escape our notice that the call to make disciples is a call to actuate a process. Discipleship is a process. It can even be a long and arduous process. It is not a one-night meeting or a weekend convention. It is a process, and a process requires *time*. So, while it is important to appropriate God's power for discipleship and appreciate God's priority and articulate God's plan for discipleship, it is also important to actuate God's process for discipleship.

This concept of process may not be palatable in our age of microwave and instant everything; instant coffee, instant food, instant hair style, "you just slap it on and go." But discipleship cannot be microwaved. The problem becomes even more critical when the process is completely waived from many churches. And so, many churches make converts but not disciples.

I have come to appreciate that churches need to have an established process to help believers to grow from babes to mature reproducing believers.

In underscoring the importance of process in discipleship, Thom Rainer and Eric Geiger say:

> God chose to create the universe in a sequential and orderly process. He also designed his creation maturation, including man to occur in process. Spiritual Growth (sanctification) is the process of a believer being transformed into the image of Christ.[20]

Discipleship is so important a task that it cannot be left to chance. The mandate to make disciples includes "teaching them to observe all things that I have commanded you." To accomplish this, we need to be deliberate, intentional, and even systematic. If that approach is not adopted in discipleship, important elements of the process can be omitted. This would result in a deficiency in the disciple, like a body that is lacking in important nutrients and suffers from the deficiency. Imagine the sense of fulfillment that Paul had when he was able to say to the Ephesian church: "I have not shunned to declare to you the whole counsel of God" (Acts 20:27).

In this chapter, I would like to share a process of discipleship that captures the important elements of disciples. This process has been influenced by some of the literature on discipleship, in particular, the books *The Master Plan of Evangelism*, by Robert Coleman, and *Discipleshift*, by Jim Putman.

This proposal is a five-part process of discipleship: connecting, consolidating, cultivating, coaching, and commissioning. This process is also modeled on the life of Christ. I will now give attention to each of these steps.

Connecting

In this age of the internet, everyone wants to be connected. Without connection you cannot browse, email, or even talk, in some instances. Well, the process of connecting is fundamental and foundational for discipleship. This is the deliberate and intentional act of establishing relationships with the aim of making disciples. This may take the disciple maker out of his or her comfort zone to share the gospel with others, especially if the person grew up in church circles or has been saved for a while. But we must make a deliberate effort to develop relationships with persons who are unsaved so that we can do our discipleship in authentic relationships. This process was so important for Jesus that he left heaven and came to earth so that he could reach fallen humanity. This is what Robert Coleman calls incarnation stage. As we seek to make disciples of Jesus Christ, we must be prepared to incarnate ourselves into the experiences of others so that we can connect with them. This cannot be artificial or superficial. We must have genuine interest in people. No wonder Jesus was referred to as the "friend of publicans and sinners" (Matthew 11:19). He reminds us that he did not come to call the righteous but sinners to repentance (Luke 5:32). We must remember that the gospel of salvation is for sinners, and we may have to cross barriers to connect with sinners.

Sometimes we are so conditioned by our clichés and religious culture that we repel sinners instead of attract them. As ministers of the gospel of Jesus Christ, we often must make deliberate choices and changes to reach people. We may even have to make personal sacrifices to connect with people. Also, God often provides opportunities for us to serve persons and bless them so that we can connect with them. Jesus often ministered to the physical needs of persons so that he might get their attention and ultimately minister to their spiritual needs. Is there anything that the Lord has put in your life that could help you to genuinely connect with persons and show the love of Christ to them? I believe that the Lord is constantly orchestrating divine appointments so that we may connect with prospective disciples. This is true for individual believers as well as local churches. To connect lovingly with persons, we must be prepared to be like the apostle Paul who says:

> For though I am free from all *men,* I have made myself a servant to all, that I might win the more; and to the Jews I became as a Jew, that I might win Jews; to those *who are* under the law, as under the law, that I might win those *who are* under the law; to those *who are* without law, as without law (not being without law toward God, but under law toward Christ), that I might win those *who are* without law; to the weak I became as weak, that I might win the weak. I have become all things to all *men,* that I might by all means save some. Now this I do for the gospel's sake, that I may be partaker of it with *you.* (1 Corinthians 9:19–23)

What unique opportunity has the Lord given to your church so that you may connect with people? For Jesus to connect with fishermen, he went by the sea. For Jesus to have connected with publicans, he went to a party hosted by a publican. If we are fishermen, we must go where the fishes are. Where will you go in the name of Christ to reach people for Jesus Christ? Remember the Great Commission includes going. We cannot wait for the sinners to come. We must *go.* We must take the initiative.

As we seek to deliberately connect with persons for discipleship, I would offer three guidelines: be sensible, be strategic, and be sensitive to the Spirit.

We need to be sensible in establishing relationships for discipleship so that we do not unnecessarily expose ourselves to temptation or danger. For example, a good guideline is to mentor persons of your own gender. In any case, you must be aware of your own strengths and weaknesses. This self- awareness is so important because we must take heed to ourselves and the doctrine (1 Timothy 4:16).

In establishing discipleship relationships, we must also be strategic. Because we have limited time and material resources, we must be faithful stewards of all with which God has blessed us. You will not be able to disciple everyone that needs discipleship, so you must choose wisely. Your sphere of influence is not unlimited. However, God has strategically positioned you to reach some persons. You may have a special ability, giftedness, privilege, or simply the knack to influence a particular group or sub-group. As you prayerfully consider strategy, you must consider your capability, your suitability, and your availability. You must acknowledge that you are not God's ideal for all persons and circumstances, but you are God's ideal for some. May God open your eyes that you will find God's ideal ministry focus for your life, including the persons, places, and circumstances. Has God placed a special group or people on your heart?

One fundamental principle of the church growth movement propounded by the father of the Church Growth Movement, Donald McGavran, is to give attention to places where there is receptivity. In other words, look for persons who are hungry, and disciple them. They must be receptive or else you stand the chance of wasting valuable time and resources. Church Growth specialist

Gary McIntosh has pointed out that one of Donald McGavran's contributions to missions is to bring to the fore that "openness to the gospel should control the direction of resources"[21] It is also important to consider the need for the gospel when allocating resources, as some persons have greater access to discipleship than others.

Finally, the guidelines that I have given above must be tempered with being sensitive to the Spirit of God. God is at work in this world drawing people to him, and none can come to Christ unless the Father draws them (John 6:44). So, like Jesus, we simply must discern how the Father is working and work with him (John 5:17). We must therefore allow the Spirit of God to lead us as we make disciples, and he will, because this matter of disciple making is more important to God than it is for us. This is the reason why Jesus left heaven and came to earth. This is the reason why Jesus died on the cruel cross. This is the reason why Jesus rose again from the dead. God is always at work in the world drawing people to himself. Will you be a laborer together with him?

Can you think of one person that you can disciple? Are you prepared to connect with that person genuinely so that he or she can follow you as you follow Christ?

What plans do you make for those who come to accept Jesus Christ as Savior and Lord? Our job does not come to an end when someone accepts Christ at an evangelistic crusade.

Paul expressed his understanding of the process of discipleship when he says in Colossians 1:28: "Him we preach warning every man and teaching every man in all wisdom, that we may present every man perfect in Jesus Christ." No wonder he was able to declare to the Ephesian elders: "I testify to you this day that I am innocent of the blood of all men. For I have not shunned to declare to you *the whole counsel of God*" (Acts 20:26–27, italics added).

In this connecting stage we would do well to incorporate the stages of incarnation, selection, and association as presented by Robert Coleman in the classic *The Master Plan of Evangelism.*

Consolidating: (bringing people to a place
of commitment, accepting Christ)

Having invested valuable time and resources in developing relationships for discipleship, we must bear in mind that *connecting* is not an end. We must seek to bring people to *consolidating* their faith in the Lord Jesus Christ. The relationship alone cannot save persons. They must have a personal encounter with Christ and experience the new birth. It is therefore important that disciples have a handle on the clear understanding of the gospel message. It is the word of God that brings conviction and produces faith for a person to come to Christ. There are many guides to share the gospel. For example, there is *Steps to Peace with God, Your Most Important Relationship, The Roman Road, and Evangelism Explosion.* Some Bibles are printed with markings that help persons to share the gospel fluently.

Whatever you do and however you do it, your goal should be to bring the person to consolidating faith in the risen Christ and experience the new birth. When a person professes faith in Christ and receives a basic understanding of the Christian faith, the person can be baptized. Baptism seems to be a good outward sign of consolidating faith in the Lord.

For many churches, baptism marks the end of consistent discipleship. Well, when a person is baptized, the task of discipleship is far from being over because we are not just making converts. We are making disciples who make disciples. Our goal should be to lead a disciple into maturity until that disciple starts reproducing. That takes us to the next level of discipleship: cultivating.

Cultivating: (helping them to grow in the Lord; consecration)

This stage is a deliberate effort to help believers to grow into maturity. Like all the stages, it is God who makes a person a disciple of Christ, and it is he alone who moves a person from one stage to the next. However, we are workers together with God. We are fully aware that it is God alone who can cause spiritual growth. Some will plant, some will water, but only God gives the increase (1 Corinthians 3:6–8). It is God's desire that his followers grow in grace and in the knowledge of the Lord Jesus Christ (2 Peter 3:18). This aspect of cultivating includes both doctrines and practices of the Christian faith. Disciples should not only be fed with cerebral material. Much of teaching in the church has been geared to the head as if a human is only intellect. The person is made up of intellect, emotion, and will, and all three areas must be catered to in discipleship.

Teaching is such a major part of discipleship yet in the church, teaching is often limited to the cognitive domain. Teaching must cater to the cognitive domain, the affective domain, and the psychomotor domain. Simply put, these refer to knowledge attitude and skill, respectively. Again, we can learn from the Master Teacher how he taught his disciples. He did not only appeal to their heads. He targeted their head, heart, and hands. In other words, Jesus impacted the entire life of a disciple. He literally lived with his disciples so that they could observe his life and order theirs accordingly.

In this step of the discipleship process, one needs to decide on the various doctrines that must be taught as well as the various lifestyle practices that must be inculcated in the life of the disciple. Again, many different tools can enhance the process of discipleship. One particularly good material for one-to-one discipleship is Small Circle and Xchange, developed by Pastor Steve McCoy of the 360 Church in Sarasota, Florida. An additional benefit to using this discipleship tool is that it may be accessed with a mobile application.

Coaching

The fourth step in this process is coaching. This is where the disciple is encouraged to practice what he or she has been learning. This is the apprenticeship. The disciple is encouraged to become skilled in the art of making discipleship. This is where the skills of delegation and supervision (these are two stages in Coleman's model) must be employed. Discipleship must not only include teaching but also coaching. Gary Colling says, "Coaching is the art and practice of enabling individuals and groups to move from where they are to where they want to be."[22]

Collins also cites the following definition of coaching from the *Handbook of Coaching*, by Frederic Hudson: "A coach is someone trained and devoted to guiding others into increased competence, commitment and confidence."[23]

As Christian leaders, we must gradually train persons to do what we are currently doing in ministry. We must learn the art of passing the baton. Some leaders have a major challenge in training others to do the work of the ministry. However, we must remember that the Lord has specially gifted leaders in the body of Christ to equip the saints for the work of the ministry (Ephesians 4:12). Church leaders must therefore give priority to equipping the saints to do ministry. This is the work of God, and we must never think that it is *our* work. We must prepare the body of Christ to do the work of the Lord. Sometimes leaders make two opposite mistakes in the passing of the baton. Sometimes we pass the baton before persons are ready to receive it, and the work suffers in the process. That is why the Scripture warns us not to appoint a "novice" as an elder (1 Timothy 3:6). However, the converse is also true, and somehow it seems to be more predominant. Sometimes, church leaders are reluctant to pass the baton. This reluctance leads to retardation in the work. Some even die with the baton still in their hands. In their book *Building the Body: Twelve Characteristics of a FIT CHURCH,* Gary McIntosh and Phil Stevenson underscore the importance of deliberate leadership development in the process of church growth and development. They advocate:

> Churches that are building the body value leadership development. They recognize that building new leaders increases the capacity and competency of the church. A church that intentionally works to develop leaders, both present and future, increases its *muscular strength* to face the future.[24]

Commissioning: (releasing people to make disciples)

The final step in the process of making disciples is that of commissioning people to the work. Having trained leaders, we must be willing to release them. Disciples must be given the authority to become authentic leaders. Having been called and appointed by God for ministry, we should be willing to recognize, empower, and release persons for ministry. We should be passionate about multiplying leaders. Persons must be properly recognized and released for ministry, with the prayers and support of the leadership and membership of the fellowship.

5

Assimilate God's People

Teaching them to observe all the things that I have commanded you.

—Matthew 28:20

So far, we have seen that faithful discipleship calls us to appropriate God's power, appreciate God's priority, articulate God's plan, and actuate God's process. We must also notice from the text that the commission that the Lord has given to the church is not to make converts; it is to make disciples. Therefore, the task is not completed when a person accepts Jesus Christ as personal Savior and is baptized. Discipleship involves consistent and continuous follow-up. Faithful discipleship calls us also to assimilate God's people in a context of fellowship. The text says, "teaching them to observe all things that I have commanded you" (Matthew 28:20). We cannot teach all things that the Lord has commanded in a weekend Bible conference. Discipleship requires assimilating the people of God into the local body so that they can become "rooted and grounded" in the things of God.

David Fray said, "Not following up … is the same as filling up a bath tub without first putting the stopper in the drain."[25] Although this statement was made with reference to marketing, it may be applicable to the task of following up new believers. New believers must be followed up and assimilated into the life of the church. According to Nelson Searcy and Jennifer Dykes Henson:

> Assimilation is integration into the local church as one moves from being merely a guest to become a fully engaged responsible member of the local Body of Christ.[26]

They also explain that we must:

> Encourage them to get involved in sticky situations where they will form connections with other people. The three most effective sticky situations are small groups, fun events and service teams.[27]

In fact, from the time someone visits our assemblies, we should have a system in place to connect with them and seek to intentionally disciple them. It includes how we meet them, how we greet them, how we seat them, and how we treat them. Sometimes people want to feel that they *belong* before they *believe*.

Rick Warren makes this poignant observation about assimilation in his book *The Purpose Driven Church*:

> While some relationships will spontaneously develop, the friendship factor in assimilation is too crucial to leave to chance. You can't just hope people

will make friends in church. You must encourage it,
plan for it, structure for it and facilitate it.[28]

With respect to this crucial matter of assimilation, I would
encourage us to remember the vowels: A, E, I, O, and U.

Associate

Engage

Integrate

Organize

Unite

Associate: There is no place for selfishness in the body of Christ.
We must make a deliberate effort to appreciate the diversity and be
willing to associate with each other regardless of our differences.
The sooner we accept the truth that we are all one in Christ Jesus,
the better it will be for our relationships. There is no place for pride
and prejudice among the people of God. We are all sinners saved by
grace. The Bible therefore exhorts us:

> Be of the same mind toward one another. Do not
> set your mind on high things, but associate with
> the humble. Do not be wise in your own opinion.
> (Romans 12:16 NKJ)

> Live in harmony with one another. Do not be
> haughty, but associate with the lowly. Never be wise
> in your own sight. (Romans 12:16 ESV)

Engage: Since newcomers to our churches are often reticent to
become involved, it is important that we make a conscious effort
to invite them to participate. We must make a deliberate effort to

engage the disengaged in the spirit of love. People may opt to remain aloof for various reasons. Some may be struggling with the impact of the past, or it simply may be their temperament. However, it is always a good Christian practice to entertain strangers. The Bible reminds us:

> Be not forgetful to entertain strangers: for thereby some have entertained angels unawares. (Hebrews 13:2 NKJV)

> Do not forget to show hospitality to strangers, for by so doing some people have shown hospitality to angels without knowing it. (Hebrews 13:2 NIV)

We must remember that first impressions are lasting. In an article entitled "Taking the Guesswork out of Guest Relations," Aaron Wilson lists "a welcoming attitude" as one of "the five most significant impressions that determine whether a church guest will return."[29] He asserts:

> "<u>friendliness alone</u> won't make guests return to a church, but an unwelcoming encounter is enough to send them packing.[30]

This finding is based on feedback from mystery visits to more than ten thousand worship services across the nation in a research conducted by Melanie Smollen, founder and president of Faith Perceptions.[31]

It must also be noted that engaging one another in life and ministry yields mutual benefits, for "As iron sharpens iron, So a man sharpens the countenance of his friend" (Proverbs 27:17).

Integrate: The experience of the entire church fellowship will be richer when we integrate the diversity of all its members. We must remember that we need each other, with our various gifts and talents, to fulfil God's purpose for the church. This is because that church operates as a body.

> For as we have many members in one body, but all the members do not have the same function, so we, *being* many, are one body in Christ, and individually members of one another. (Romans 12:4–5)

We must be integrally integrated so that the intention of God can be instituted. This integration must transcend physical, social, economic, racial, cultural, or any other earthly barriers. It is God's plan for people to blend their differences to reflect his glory.

Organize: Organization is of paramount importance in assimilating persons into the fellowship. If we are going to be faithful in "teaching *them* to observe all things" (italics added) we must cater to "them," for *all* of "them." "Them" come in all ages and all stages. They have different preferences and frames of reference. Because of the differences of disciples, we have to offer differentiated learning, taking the uniqueness of persons into consideration, including learning styles. In this matter of discipleship, one cap does not fit all and may not have the same shape, but it is wise for all sizes to be made of the same material. In other words, we may change form while keeping the function. For example, we may change methods while keeping the message constant. All this requires some level of organization. God requires us to ensure that all things are done decently and in order (1 Corinthians 14:40).

Also, if we are going to teach disciples "all things" that Christ has commanded, we must have some form of organization. To be faithful in teaching "all things" to disciples requires the use of curriculum with pre-determined content. We must plan the teaching in such a way that disciples learn the whole counsel of God. Without this, disciples may get an overdose of some nutrients, and even worse, a deficiency in other nutrients.

Unite: Another reason why it is important to assimilate people into the fellowship is because unity is an important foundation for the body of Christ. Jesus did not only prescribe it for his disciples, but he also prayed for it. Hear his prayer:

> My prayer is not for them alone. I pray also for those who will believe in me through their message, that all of them may be one, Father, just as you are in me and I am in you. May they also be in us so that the world may believe that you have sent me. (John 17:20–21)

Disciples are called to unite with each other not only because it resembles the relationship that exists in the Godhead, but because it has inherent evangelistic potency: "that the world may believe that you have sent me" (John 17:21).

Therefore, it is clear that the Great Commission cannot be divorced from the Great Commandments, which state:

> "The most important one," answered Jesus, is this: 'Hear, O Israel: The Lord our God, the Lord is one. Love the Lord your God with all your heart and with all your soul and with all your mind and with all your strength.' The second is this: 'Love your

neighbor as yourself.' There is no commandment greater than these." (Mark 12:29–31)

Because this matter of unity is so important to Jesus, his disciples are expected to be "endeavouring to keep the unity of the Spirit in the bond of peace" (Ephesians 4:3).

6

Accentuate God's Preeminence

Obey all things that I have commanded you.

—Matthew 28:20

The call to discipleship is a call to unswerving commitment and radical obedience to Jesus Christ. It is expected that disciples of Jesus Christ are fully surrendered to his Lordship and leadership. The statement "I have commanded you" suggests that he expects that his teachings will be followed ardently. The use of the word *obey* underscores that he has the right to tell us what to do and that he expects us to comply fully. Colossians 1:18 tells us that "He is the head of the body, the church, who is the beginning, the firstborn from the dead, that in all things He may have the pre-eminence." Disciples must fully subject themselves to the Lordship of Christ.

Disciples of Christ must be taught how to observe all things that he has commanded. The original word used here is *terein*, which means, "to observe," "to keep," "to obey." Note that the text does not only admonish us to teach disciples but to teach disciples *to obey* all things that the Master has commanded. The text says, "teaching them *to observe* all things I have commanded you" (Matthew 28:19). Disciple making requires both theory and practice. It involves unswerving commitment to practical living that resembles the life of Christ. It is not just giving information. It is effecting transformation. Jesus demands complete, exclusive, and unflinching obedience to himself. We are called to be like Christ. The Apostle John emphasized this teaching in 1 John 2:3–6:

> Now by this we know that we know Him, if we keep His commandments. He who says, "I know Him," and does not keep His commandments, is a liar, and the truth is not in him. But whoever keeps His word, truly the love of God is perfected in him. By this we know that we are in Him. He who says he abides in Him ought himself also to walk just as He walked.

Jesus calls his followers to demonstrate the Christlike life in this world. This is a call to full surrender and a consistent walk with him. He is Lord of all or none at all. He is not satisfied with partial commitment or lukewarmness. He requires our total allegiance. God must get first place in our lives. We must have no other god before him.

Jesus gave a sobering discourse about discipleship as he made his way to Jerusalem to lay down his life for the sins of the world. Luke 9:51 tells us: "Now it came to pass, when the time had come for Him to be received up, that He steadfastly set His face to go to Jerusalem." As Jesus steadfastly set his face toward the Old Jerusalem, so we must steadfastly set our face toward the New Jerusalem. Also, we must be resolute on our journey to the New Jerusalem.

Jesus was making his way to the cross. He gave the following teaching about discipleship.

Let us consider Luke 14:25. The Bible says, "there were great crowds going along with Him." The crowd was with Jesus along the road to Jerusalem. But he wanted the crowd to understand something about that road. He wanted the crowd to learn a thing or two about the way of the cross. He wanted to eliminate any misconception about following him. The Bible says he turned and said to them:

> "If anyone comes to Me and does not hate his father and mother, wife and children, brothers and sisters, yes, and his own life also, he cannot be My disciple. And whoever does not bear his cross and come after Me cannot be My disciple. For which of you, intending to build a tower, does not sit down first and count the cost, whether he has enough to finish it—lest, after he has laid the foundation, and is not able to finish, all who see it begin to mock him, saying, 'This man began to build and was not able to finish.'? Or what king, going to make war against another king, does not sit down first and consider whether he is able with ten thousand to meet him who comes against him with twenty thousand? Or else, while the other is still a great way off, he sends a delegation and asks conditions of peace. So likewise, whoever of you does not forsake all that he has cannot be My disciple." (Luke 14:26–33)

In this passage Jesus identifies three broad categories that can present a challenge to faithful discipleship.

People

This passage is not to encourage discord in families. Jesus was simply underscoring that people must not come between him and his followers. He says, "If anyone comes to Me and does not hate his father and mother, wife and children, brothers and sisters, yes, and his own life also, he cannot be My disciple" (Luke 14:26). All relationships must be relegated to a secondary place as Jesus takes first place in the lives of disciples. Sometimes our closest relationships are our greatest challenge to following Jesus. In many areas of the world, persons are ostracized by family and friends when they choose to follow Jesus. People may fall into different categories, but some of the people may include family, friends, or foes. Some people who love us may hinder us from following Christ by encouraging us to choose what looks best for us and presents the least pain and the most pay. Others may unwittingly instill fear in us by telling us about the dangers that make us vulnerable. The Pharisees tried to intimidate Jesus by telling him that Herod was going to kill him in Jerusalem. But Jesus was not intimidated by the threat of danger for he knew that his Father was in control.

Personal Well-Being

Another category in which we can be hindered from following Christ is in the pursuit of our personal well-being. It is great to seek personal well-being. So, what does it mean when Jesus says that unless we hate our life, we cannot be his disciples? It is pointing out that our selfish ambitions, aspirations, and pursuits must be secondary to following

Jesus. Sometimes, to experience God's ideal for our lives we must deny ourselves. Matthew 6:24–26 puts it this way:

> Then Jesus said to His disciples, "If anyone desires to come after Me, let him deny himself, and take up his cross, and follow Me. For whoever desires to save his life will lose it, but whoever loses his life for My sake will find it. For what profit is it to a man if he gains the whole world, and loses his own soul? Or what will a man give in exchange for his soul?

Following Jesus' calls for self-denial, we must often deny ourselves of pleasure, power, popularity, or possessions. Sometimes we even need to lay down our own will on the altar to follow Christ. Jesus had to do it to follow his Father. On his journey to the cross, he stopped in the garden of Gethsemane and prayed until his sweat became like drops of blood. What was his prayer?

> Then Jesus came with them to a place called Gethsemane, and said to the disciples, "Sit here while I go and pray over there." And he took with him Peter, and the two sons of Zebedee, and he began to be sorrowful and deeply distressed. Then he said to them, "My soul is exceedingly sorrowful, even to death. Stay here and watch with Me." He went a little farther and fell on his face and prayed, saying, "O My Father, if it is possible, let this cup pass from Me; nevertheless, not as I will, but as You will." (Matthew 26: 36–39)

The call to follow Jesus Christ is a call to total surrender, regardless of the consequences.

Not even our personal comfort or security must stand in the way. The Centre for the Study of Global Christianity at Gordon-Conwell Theological Seminary estimates that one hundred thousand Christians are martyred annually.[32] The journey to Jerusalem is not easy, but it is worth it.

We must not fear those who can destroy the body but cannot touch the soul. We must rather fear him that can destroy both body and soul in hell (Matthew 10:28).

I believe that the world is now entering a new season in which the persecution of those who follow Christ will become more extensive as well as more intensive. We must be prepared to be imprisoned or imperiled because of our allegiance to Jesus. Persecution may be new for Christians in the West, but it is a common experience for believers in many countries today. And the history of the church is replete with the persecution of the saints.

We must remember that the servant is not above his master, and what they did to Jesus they may do to those who follow Jesus. It was not easy for Jesus. It was not easy for the disciples. It was not easy for the early church. It has not been easy for believers throughout the centuries. We should not expect it to be easy for us. But it will be worth it because the alternative is disastrous. John 15 says:

> "If the world hates you, you know that it hated
> Me before it hated you. If you were of the world,
> the world would love its own. Yet because you are
> not of the world, but I chose you out of the world,
> therefore the world hates you. Remember the word
> that I said to you, 'A servant is not greater than
> his master.' If they persecuted Me, they will also

persecute you. If they kept My word, they will keep
yours also. But all these things they will do to you
for My name's sake, because they do not know Him
who sent Me."

Possession

The third category that may present hindrances to faithfully
following Jesus Christ is our possessions. Our attitude to possession
can stand in the way of our walk with the Lord. Jesus says:

> So likewise, whoever of you does not forsake all that
> he has cannot be My disciple. (Luke 14:33)

Do not misunderstand me. It is not sinful to have possessions—
even great possessions. Job was rich. Abraham was rich. Many of
the Lord's servants have been blessed with the wealth of this world.
However, possessions must not stand in the way of following Jesus.
The desire for possessions caused Judas to sell out Jesus for thirty
pieces of silver. The rich young ruler went away sorrowful because
he was not willing to part with his possessions to follow Christ.
Many are kept out of the kingdom because of wealth, or rather, the
desire for wealth. Paul gave Timothy some wise instructions about
possessions:

> Now godliness with contentment is great gain.
> For we brought nothing into *this* world, *and it is*
> certain we can carry nothing out. And having food
> and clothing, with these we shall be content. But
> those who desire to be rich fall into temptation and
> a snare, and *into* many foolish and harmful lusts
> which drown men in destruction and perdition.

> For the love of money is a root of all *kinds of* evil,
> for which some have strayed from the faith in their
> greediness, and pierced themselves through with
> many sorrows. (1 Timothy 6:6–10)

Having seen some of the challenges that may prevent persons from being faithful disciples should put us on caution; we will now look at some guidelines that Jesus gave to help us to be faithful disciples. These are also based on the passage in Luke 14:26–33.

These guidelines are to carry the cross, count the cost, and complete the course.

Carry the Cross

In Luke 14:27 Jesus says, "And whoever does not bear his cross and come after Me cannot be My disciple." If we are going to be faithful followers of Jesus Christ, we must be prepared to carry our cross. Jesus tells us clearly as he was on the way to the cross that if we are planning to follow him, we must also be prepared to go the way of the cross. It was on the cross that he won victory for himself and the entire human race. We must not forget that there is glory in the cross. Jesus endured the cross and despised the shame before he sat down at the right hand of the Father (Hebrews 12:33). We must endure the cross now; later we will receive the crown. In this fallen world we must be prepared to endure hardships. We are pilgrims and strangers (1 Peter 1:1) so we must not expect to be at home in this world.

The Bible tells us that "all that will live godly in Christ Jesus shall suffer persecution" (2 Timothy 3:12). There is no Christianity without the cross. Whatever comes our way, we must persevere for we are soldiers of the cross. The COVID-19 challenges in 2020 and 2021 have caused many to acknowledge that we are in the last days and that the last days are characterized by "perilous times." As the coming of Christ draws closer, we must be prepared for persecution, whatever form it may take. Jesus tells us in Matthew 5:11–12:

> Blessed are you when they revile and persecute you, and say all kinds of evil against you falsely for My sake. Rejoice and be exceedingly glad, for great is your reward in heaven, for so they persecuted the prophets who were before you.

Count the Cost

Following Jesus Christ does not only require us to carry our cross but also to count the cost.

Luke 14:28 says,

> For which of you, intending to build a tower, does not sit down first and count the cost.

Following Christ is costly. But count the cost. Someone has said that if you think obedience is costly, try disobedience. Think today what else is more profitable than following Christ.

> For what will it profit a man if he gains the whole world, and loses his own soul? Or what will a man give in exchange for his soul? For whoever is ashamed of Me and My words in this adulterous and sinful generation, of him the Son of Man also will be ashamed when He comes in the glory of His Father with the holy angels. (Mark 8:36–38)

Count the cost! Following Christ is going to cost you. What are you willing to give up to faithfully follow Christ? It may cost you a relationship that is dishonorable to the Lord. It may cost you your job. It may cost you fame and fortune. Count the cost! What shall a man give in exchange for his soul?

Complete the Course

If following Christ involves carrying the cross and counting the cost, I would also suggest to us that it also involves completing the course. Jesus calls us to endure to the end. Jesus says that a man building a tower must calculate the cost to complete it lest he lays the foundation and is unable to finish it. In other words, following Christ means staying the course to the end. We are called to "press toward the mark for the prize of the high calling of God in Christ Jesus" (Philippians 3:14, KJV).

No one who has put his hands to the plow and draws back is worthy of him (Luke 9:62). I find it interesting that the kingdom of God is compared to a sower who went out to sow seeds. The seed, which is the word of God, fell on four different kinds of soil. What soil are you? Hear how Jesus explains this parable in Luke 8:

> This is the meaning of the parable: The seed is the word of God. Those along the path are the ones who hear, and then the devil comes and takes away the word from their hearts, so that they may not believe and be saved. Those on the rocky ground are the ones who receive the word with joy when they hear it, but they have no root. They believe for a while, but in the time of testing they fall away. The seed that fell among thorns stands for those who hear, but as they go on their way they are choked by

life's worries, riches and pleasures, and they do not mature. But the seed on good soil stands for those with a noble and good heart, who hear the word, retain it, and by persevering produce a crop (Luke 8:11-15, NIV).

It is very sobering to note that only the good soil produces fruit. Again, I ask, what soil are you?

You cannot stop part way. God calls his disciples to go the full way for we shall be known by our fruits.

We cannot afford to stop now. We have come too far to turn back now. If you have stopped following the Lord, it is time to repent and return to that place from which you have fallen. The Lord will abundantly pardon. That is what the death of Jesus Christ is all about: the forgiveness of sins.

Can you remember singing songs like, "I have decided to follow Jesus no turning back, no turning back?"

Following Jesus is a one-way street. No U-turn is allowed. Reversing is not allowed. Stopping is not allowed. We must be unwavering in our commitment.

> Therefore, my beloved brethren, be steadfast, immovable, always abounding in the work of the Lord, knowing that your labor is not in vain in the Lord. (1 Corinthians 15:58)

The journey to Jerusalem was not easy for Jesus, but it was worth it. Our journey to the New Jerusalem will not be easy, but it is worth it. Matthew 7:13 says,

> Enter by the narrow gate; for wide is the gate and broad is the way that leads to destruction, and there

are many who go in by it. Because narrow is the gate
and difficult is the way which leads to life, and there
are few who find it.

As we close this chapter, we see that the Great Commission calls
us to accentuate God's preeminence in the lives of his disciples. This
is aptly summed up by the following statement:

Jesus' call to discipleship is an all-or-nothing
summons, reaching into every area of our lives. It
involves giving him pre-eminence over the closest
of our human relationships and over the desires we
have for our lives. In short, it involves becoming his
servant in the world and giving your life to that end.
Paradoxically we give up that which we cannot keep
to gain that which we cannot lose. If we don't, we
lose all in the end (cf. Matthew 16:25).[33]

We praise the Lord that he who calls us is faithful and can keep
us to the end for we are kept by the power of God.

Now to Him who is able to keep you from stumbling,

And to present *you* faultless

Before the presence of His glory with exceeding joy,

To God our Savior,

Who alone is wise,

Be glory and majesty,

Dominion and power,

Both now and forever.

Amen. (Jude 24–25)

7

Anticipate God's Presence

And lo, I am with you always, even to the end of
the age.

—Matthew 28:20

We have observed that Jesus began the Great Commission by
asserting His supremacy. It is noteworthy also that Jesus closed
the Great Commission by assuring his disciples of his perpetual
presence in discipleship. Therefore, as we carry out the task of
making disciples, we must anticipate his manifest presence.

So, we recall that faithful discipleship calls us to appropriate
God's power, appreciate God's priority, articulate God's plan,
actuate God's process, and assimilate God's people. Finally, we add
that we must also anticipate God's presence. If he promised to be
with us, then we can expect to experience his presence in the process
of discipleship.

We must minister with the consciousness that discipleship is God's business, and that God will take care of his business.

Discipleship is God's heartbeat. This is not something that we have thought about and are asking God to help us with. Discipleship is God's plan, and it is he who invites us to join him in this task, so he is in it fully with us, working mysteriously and supernaturally to execute it and expand it.

From the dawn of creation, it has been God's desire to share intimacy with humanity, the masterpiece of his creation. When God created human beings in the garden of Eden, it was his joy to come down and commune with humankind. The Bible tells us in Genesis 3:8 that "they heard the sound of the Lord God walking in the garden in the cool of the day and Adam and his wife hid themselves from the presence of the Lord God." This passage indicates that Adam and Eve heard a familiar sound, and they knew it was the presence of God. However, after they had sinned, they were evading the presence of the Lord instead of enjoying the presence of him. Sin had formed a barrier between God and humans, but God continued to pursue humankind and restore the relationship so that man can once again enjoy the presence of God. We see this concept being developed throughout the scriptures.

During their sojourn in the wilderness, the Lord assured his people of his divine presence with the pillar of fire by night and the pillar of cloud by day.

> And the LORD went before them by day in a pillar of cloud to lead the way, and by night in a pillar of fire to give them light, so as to go by day and night. He did not take away the pillar of cloud by day or the pillar of fire by night *from* before the people. (Exodus 13:21–22)

He commanded Moses to make a tabernacle to entertain his presence. At times, the presence of the Lord flooded the tabernacle so that the people just fell prostrate before the presence of the living God (Exodus 25:1–40:38).

When the children of Israel entered the promised land, God commanded David to prepare to build a temple to host his presence. This temple was subsequently built and dedicated to the Lord by Solomon. At the dedication of the temple, the presence of the Lord was manifested with such glory that not even the priests could minister. Everyone was struck by the awesome presence of God. After the destruction of the temple and the exile, God commanded his people to rebuild the temple. He desperately desires to live among his people.

The Old Testament prophets spoke about the new dispensation in which God would establish a new covenant with his people. Germane to this new covenant is the presence of God taking up residence in humans. Ezekiel prophesied: "I will put My Spirit within you and cause you to walk in My statutes, and you will keep My judgments and do *them*" (Ezekiel 36:27; Jeremiah 31). God continues to unfold his plan to dwell with humankind.

This took on new dimensions when Jesus came to the earth to dwell among humanity in bodily form. John describes this when he said that the Word became flesh and dwelt amongst us (John 1:14). Jesus lived with humanity for three and a half years, and then he returned to the Father. Yet, he did not withdraw his presence from humankind. He made his presence available to all believers personally when he poured out the Holy Spirit. The Holy Spirit took up residence in the lives of all followers of Christ. Jesus had promised his disciples that he would send the Holy Spirit to abide with them forever (John 14:16). It is God's desire to dwell with humanity. He wants people to be thoroughly convinced that he will always be with them. Jesus cautioned his followers not to hit the road until they were endued with power from on high. Acts 2 records how the disciples were filled with the Holy Ghost and ministered powerfully in the power of God. The Holy Spirit was given to fill humanity with God's divine presence and power to accomplish the work of God (Acts 1:8). The Holy Spirit is also a guarantee that we shall live in the fuller presence of God (Ephesians 4:30; 2 Corinthians 2:21–22). This fuller presence will be experienced in the future. Revelation 21:3–4 tells us:

> And I heard a loud voice from heaven saying, "Behold, the tabernacle of God *is* with men, and He will dwell with them, and they shall be His people. God Himself will be with them *and be* their God. And God will wipe away every tear from their eyes; there shall be no more death, nor sorrow, nor crying. There shall be no more pain, for the former things have passed away."

So, we see that from creation to consummation it is God's plan to be with his people.

Therefore, as we make disciples of Jesus Christ, we can be assured of the promised presence of God with us. We must then anticipate that presence to minister as we make disciples. He will never leave you or forsake you. Even when the devil shows up, God will show up even greater. Do not be afraid. Trust God. He is *Jehovah Shama*, the God who is there. Will you therefore go and make disciples in the mighty presence of the Living God?

Now, are you prepared to live eternally in the presence of God? Are you prepared to go to heaven when you die, or when the Lord returns? If you are *not* ready, the good news is that you can *get* ready today. You can pray this simple prayer and ask Jesus to come into your heart.

Dear God,

I realize that I am a sinner, and I cannot save myself. But I believe that Jesus died to pay the penalty of my sins and rose again from the dead to give me the gift of eternal life. Today I receive this gift from you. Please forgive me of all my sins and make me a new person. In Jesus's name I pray, amen.

If you have prayed that prayer, you can be assured that you are now a child of God (St. John 1:12).

If you are already a child of God and assured of eternal salvation, I invite you to pray another prayer, making yourself available to God to make disciples. This prayer is found in Isaiah 1:8. When Isaiah heard the voice of God asking, "Whom shall I send, and who will go for us?" He answered, "Here am I; send me." Will you pray that prayer today?

"Here am I; send me" (Isaiah 1:8)

Go in the power and presence of the triune God to make disciples of Jesus Christ, who is the way, the truth, and the life (John 14:6).

He who has the Son has life; he who does not have the Son of God does not have life. (1 John 5:12)

CONCLUSION

In this book we have tried to share the essence of the Great Commission. However, as stated at the outset, the intention of this initiative was never to simply provide information. It is to effect transformation and enlist participation in the task of making disciples of Jesus Christ. Demystifying discipleship should result in *doing* discipleship. As we become better disciples and better disciple makers, let us pray fervently that we will faithfully:

Appropriate God's power

Appreciate God's priority

Articulate God's plan

Actuate God's plan

Actuate God's process

Assimilate God's people

Accentuate God's preeminence

Like the apostle Paul prayed for the church at Colossae, I pray "that you may walk worthy of the Lord, fully pleasing *Him,* being fruitful in every good work and increasing in the knowledge of God" (Colossians 1:10).

ENDNOTES

1   Allen Yeh, *Poly-Centric Missiology: Twenty-First Century Missions from Everyone to Everywhere* (Downers Grove: Intervarsity Press, 2016).

2   Mission from everywhere to everywhere (christiantoday.com) accessed March 9, 2021.

3   Jim Putman, *Discipleshift: Five Steps that Help your Church to make Disciples that make Disciples* (Grand Rapids, MI: Zondervan, 2013).

4   https://bible.org/seriespage/2-understanding-meaning-term-disciple, accessed November 12, 2020.

5   https://dictionary.cambridge.org/dictionary/english/disciple, accessed November 12, 2020.

6   Discipleship: Biblical Definition, History, What It is Today (justdisciple.com) accessed March 29, 2021.

7   Who are the Navigators? | GotQuestions.org

8   https://www.navigators.org/wp-content/uploads/2019/01/navtool-word-hand.pdf, accessed November 12, 2020.

9   Some of these words were taken from Evangelical Training Association text entitled "Your Ministry of Evangelism," by Elmer Towns, (Wheaton, IL: Evangelical Training Association, 1991, 2002), 7–8.

10 https://sweetslyrics.com/heritage-singers/champion-of-love-lyrics.

11 https://www.biblestudytools.com/dictionary/authority/.

12 Paul Borthwick, *Great Commission Great Compassion* (Downers Grove: Inter Varsity Press, 2015), 32.

13 Joe Wyrostek, *Disciples that Make Disciples* (Chicago: Metro Praise International Publishing, 2006), 80.

14 Winfield Bevins, *Marks of a Movement: What the Church Today Can Learn from the Wesleyan Revival* (Grand Rapids, MI: Zondervan, 2019), 99.

15 https://evangelismexplosion.org/about-us/history/, accessed November 27, 2020.

16 16 https://evangelismexplosion.org/about-us/history/ accessed November 27, 2020.

17 https://joshuaproject.net/assets/media/handouts/status-of-world-evangelization.pdf, "Status of World Evangelization 2020," accessed November 27, 2020.

18 For a more comprehensive overview, Walter Kaiser's book *The Promise Plan of God: A Biblical Theology of the Old and New Testament* (Zondervan Academic, 2008).

19 https://joshuaproject.net/assets/media/handouts/status-of-world-evangelization.pdf, "Status of World Evangelization 2020," accessed November 27, 2020.

20 Thom Rainer and Eric Geiger, *Simple Church: Returning to God's Process for Making Disciples (Nashville, TN: B&H Publishing)*, 2011.

21 Gary McIntosh, Donald

22 Gary Collins, *Christian Coaching: Helping Others Turn Potential into reality* (Colorado Springs: Navpress, 2009).

23 Ibid,

24 Gary McIntosh and Phil Stevenson, *Building the Body: 12 Characteristics of a FIT CHURCH* (Grand Rapids, MI: Baker Publishing, 2018), 111.

25 Follow-Up Marketing: How to Win More Sales with Less Effort (busi-nessknowhow.com), January 11, 2017, accessed December 1, 2020.

26 Nelson Searsy and Jennifer Dykes Henson, *Fusion: Turning First Time Guests into Fully Engaged Members of Your Church.* (Grand Rapids, MI: Baker Books, 2017), 14

27 Ibid.

28 Rick Warren, *The Purpose Driven Church: Growth Without Compromising Your Message and Mission.* (Grand Rapids, MI: Zondervan, 1995), 324.

29 5 Things That Matter Most to Church Visitors | Facts & Trends (factsandtrends.net), accessed December 3, 2020.

30 5 Things That Matter Most to Church Visitors | Facts & Trends (factsandtrends.net) accessed December 3, 2020.

[31] 5 Things That Matter Most to Church Visitors | Facts & Trends (factsandtrends.net) accessed December 3, 2020.

[32] 50thbookletFINAL.pdf (gordonconwell.edu) accessed March 3, 2021.

[33] https://bible.org/seriespage/2-understanding-meaning-term-disciple.

WORKS CITED

Books

Bevins, Winfield. *Marks of a Movement: What the Church today Can Learn from the Wesleyan Revival.* Grand Rapids, MI: Zondervan, 2019.

Borthwick, Paul. *Great Commission Great Compassion.* Downers Grove: Inter Varsity Press, 2012.

Collins, Gary. *Christian Coaching: Helping Others Turn Potential into Reality.* Colorado Springs: Navpress, 2009.

McIntosh, Gary, and Phil Stevenson. *Building the Body: 12 Characteristics of a FIT CHURCH.* Grand Rapids, MI: Baker Publishing, 2018.

McIntoch, Gary. *Donald A. McGavran: A Biography of the Twentieth Century's Premier Missiologist.* New York: Church Leaders Insights, 2015.

Putman, Jim, and Bobby Harrington. *Discipleshift: Five Steps that Help Your Church to make Disciples that Make Disciples.* Grand Rapids, MI: Zondervan, 2013.

Rainer, Thom, and Eric Geiger. *Simple Church: Returning to God's Process for Making Disciples*. Nashville, TN: B&H Publishing, 2011.

Searcy, Nelson, and Jennifer Dykes Henson. *Fusion: Turning First Time Guests into Fully Engaged Members of Your Church*. Grand Rapids, MI: Baker Books, 2017.

Towns, Elmer. *Your Ministry of Evangelism*. Wheaton, IL: Evangelical Training Association, 1991, 2002.

Warren, Rick. *The Purpose Driven Church: Growth Without Compromising Your Message and Mission*. Grand Rapids, MI: Zondervan, 1995.

Wyrostek, Joe. *Disciples that Make Disciples*. Chicago: Metro Praise International, 2006.

Yeh, Allen. Poly-Centric Missiology: *Twenty-First Century Missions From Everyone to Everywhere*. Downers Grove: Intervarsity Press, 2016.

Websites

https://bible.org/seriespage/2-understanding-meaning-term-disciple.

https://dictionary.cambridge.org/dictionary/english/disciple.

https://www.navigators.org/wp-content/uploads/2019/01/navtool-word-hand.pdf.

https://evangelismexplosion.org/about-us/history/.

Follow-Up Marketing: How to Win More Sales with Less Effort (businessknowhow.com).

https://joshuaproject.net/assets/media/handouts/status-of-world-evangelization.pdf.

https://www.biblestudytools.com/dictionary/authority/.
5 Things That Matter Most to Church Visitors | Facts & Trends (factsandtrends.net).

https://bible.org/seriespage/2-understanding-meaning-term-disciple.
Discipleship: Biblical Definition, History, What It is Today (justdisciple.com).
Who are the Navigators? | GotQuestions.org

ABOUT THE AUTHOR

Dr. Raphael Thomas is the president of Blessing Basket International, a missions organization that he cofounded with his wife, Velda, in 2017. He also currently serves as director of missions and evangelism at the Germantown Christian Assembly, Philadelphia.

Dr. Thomas and his wife served the Lord in Jamaica for over thirty years in full-time Christian ministry before they relocated to the United States in 2020. Dr. Thomas served as pastor of the Annotto Bay Gospel Chapel, St. Mary, Jamaica, for thirty-two years. He also served as chairman of the Gospel Chapel Education Centre, which he was instrumental in founding in 1990. He is a former chairman and executive director of the North-Eastern Missionary Conference, a fellowship of thirty-three Christian Brethren Assemblies in Jamaica. Raphael continues to serve on various boards in Jamaica, including Gospel Chapel Education Centre, Midland Bible Institute, Choose Life International, and North-Eastern Missionary Conference.

Raphael holds a doctor of ministry from Columbia Theological Seminary, a doctor of clinical Christian counseling from Central Christian University, a master of arts from the Caribbean Graduate School of Theology, a bachelor of arts in theology from the Jamaica Theological Seminary, a diploma in teaching from the University of the West Indies (through Shortwood Teachers' College), and he is also a graduate of Haggai Institute (now Haggai International), of which he now serves as an international facilitator.

Dr. Thomas has been an Adjunct Lecturer at the Caribbean Graduate School of Theology since 2001 where he taught the courses Caribbean Evangelism, Dynamics of Church Growth, Biblical and Theological Themes in Counseling, Theology of Missions, Latter Prophets and Writings, Pentateuch and Former Prophets, Pastoral Care and Counseling and Biblical and Theological Themes in Counseling.

Raphael has a passion for preaching and teaching the Word of God. He has spoken at Evangelistic Crusades, Bible Conventions, Christian Camps, and Mission Conferences. He carries a burden for Global Evangelization.

In 2003 he was certified as a behavioral consultant with the Institute for Motivational Living. He is a licensed clinical pastoral counselor with the National Christian Counselors Association. In 2017 he received a National Award from the Prime Minister of Jamaica for his contribution to education.

In 1984, while he was still a teenager, Raphael was named the Year of the Bible Personality for emerging as the champion in the

Jamaica Youth for Christ Year of the Bible Competition. In that competition, Raphael memorized and recited eleven hundred verses of scripture (one-eighth of the New Testament) and won a trip to Israel and Jordan.

On many occasions, Raphael has fasted for revival, sometimes for periods lasting forty days. He shares this passion for revival in his book *Biblical Dynamics for Revival Today: Studies in the Life of King Hezekiah.*

In 1992, Raphael and his wife were commended to the work of the Lord by the Annotto Bay Gospel Chapel in association with the North-Eastern Missionary Conference, a regional body of the Christian Brethren Assemblies Jamaica (CBAJ). Their commendation statues were endorsed by the Germantown Christian Assembly (GCA) in 2020, thus recognizing them as missionaries in North-America as well, where they serve with GCA and Blessing Basket International to share the gospel locally and globally. They have two adult sons, Timothy and Nathanael, both of whom are actively engaged in Christian ministry.

L - R, Timothy, Raphael, Velda, Nathanael

Printed in the United States
by Baker & Taylor Publisher Services